Youth in a changing society

YOUTH IN A CHANGING SOCIETY

Fred Milson

Head of Youth and Community Service Department
Westhill College of Education, Birmingham

Routledge & Kegan Paul

London and Boston

First published 1972
by Routledge & Kegan Paul Ltd.
Broadway House, 68-74 Carter Lane,
London EC4V 5EL
and 9 Park Street, Boston, Mass. 02108, U.S.A.
Printed in Great Britain by
Ebenezer Baylis & Son Limited,
The Trinity Press, Worcester, and London
ISBN 0 7100 7204 X

To Irene Dyson

For many years
A good friend and an efficient secretary

45791

Contents

Contents

Introduction

In most human societies the young are a source of perennial interest and hence of continuing conversation.

Socrates wrote of them in the fourth century B.C., 'They have execrable manners, flaunt authority, have no respect for their elders. What kind of awful creatures will they become when they grow up?' Incongruously perhaps we may place at the side of the philosopher's comment the struggles between the generations which sometimes occur in the Western films when the Red Indian braves want to overthrow the authority of the ancient chief.

The question of youth has been a dominant theme for outstanding English writers. One thinks immediately of Shakespeare's *Hamlet* and Dickens's *David Copperfield*. In the index of the *Oxford Dictionary of Quotations*, there are 116 entries under the heading of 'youth' and this is taking no account of related quotations under 'young' and 'youthful'. As is to be expected they refer to comments which reflect every mood. There is cynicism: 'Youth is a blunder' (Disraeli). There is educational insight: 'Youth, what man's age is like to be doth show: We may our ends by our beginnings know' (Sir John Denham). There is delight and confidence: 'Youth, beauty, graceful action seldom fail' (John Dryden). There is pity: 'Youth is the season of credulity' (William Pitt). There is the hedonistic approach: 'Youth's the season made for joys, Love is then our duty' (John Gay). There is the cautionary comment: 'It is good for a man that he bear the yoke in his youth' (The Bible: Lamentations). When men sing about youth, they comment on all the grandeur and squalor, all the hope and pathos of life.

It certainly cannot be supposed that there has been any decline in this interest during the last twenty years. On the contrary, the young and their activities have become one of our major preoccupations and with some of us, at certain times, almost an obsession. The activities of the young today are international news and often dominate our newspapers and television screens. No sooner are we forgetting the work of the Red Guards than we are constantly reminded of trouble on the American college campus. In Britain today one of the most successful conversational gambits is, 'And what do you think about the young people?'

The reasons for this unfailing interest are both obvious and complex. Alike for individual older people and societies as a whole, the young constitute a direct threat and the most important promise. In them we may be fulfilled or by them we may be destroyed. Hence the fact that 'youth' is a highly emotional subject and to the young we develop ambivalent attitudes.

For us as individuals, the young are a threat because they will replace us in positions of power: they have the one incomparable asset which we have lost – years to live and time to change their circumstances; their presence gives rise to feelings of nostalgia and regret and guilt; they disturb our settled views and invade our private value systems. But on the other hand, they are 'our young people', perhaps in the biological, family sense, but if not, by association in our minds, with those who are united to us by blood: they appeal to us by their *naïveté* and helplessness; their lack of experience often gives them an optimism which has not been tested; they do not realize how painful is pain and how intractable is evil; and yet we recognize in them a hope for a better future.

Societies too see youngsters as a threat mainly because they unite in themselves the two greatest psychological and biological forces which 'by their very universality and vitality, present civilized man with his most baffling problems: namely, sexuality and aggression'.[1] They are less disposed to accept the *status quo*, having less of a stake in the society as it is: they threaten the established structures of meaning, value, authority and power. Societies approach their young functionally: there are strong systems of socialization for the young though these systems may be covert and heavily disguised or overt and frankly avowed. Societies have three distinct but related purposes with their young:

1 To communicate culture (using the word in its sociological meaning as the established way of life of a definable community and a way of life which has to be learned by newcomers if they are to be socially-acceptable).
2 To perpetuate through the young, a recognizable identity for the community. This is part of what is happening when children in American schools begin the day by saluting the flag.
3 To gain their support for existing structures of power and thus to mobilize them to resist change.

But it would be altogether too cynical to consider that the whole interest of all societies is functional: part of it is humane and compassionate. For example, in the USSR. a common reaction among older people is that they would like the younger generation to enjoy life more than *they* did in the years of austerity when consumer's needs were sacrificed to the demands of national economic growth. And this motivation is reflected in educational programmes. In most civilized communities, there are organized expressions of the desires of many adult people that the youngsters should have a chance 'to make the most of themselves'.

However, the perennial interest of individuals and societies in their young is often an example of 'zeal without knowledge': public opinion – largely guided by hearsay and prejudices and addicted to stereotyped images – is often wrong in estimating the habits, attitudes and social position of young people in contemporary Britain. This is more disastrous, as we shall see, at a time of rapid social change. In this respect, the question of youth in our community does not differ from that of other major social issues of our time.

On the one hand, we have a growing volume of sociological knowledge which, widely known and used, could help us to be less at the mercy of events. Man could climb into the saddle of power aided by the social sciences as well as by technology. But this knowledge tends to remain the private preserve of professional sociologists. One major reason is that the professional sociologists have never attended to the business of communication: they will not simplify their words or their concepts for popular consumption. (They are inclined to ask 'Is your maternal progenitor cognizant of your absence from the domiciliary residence?' when they mean, 'Does your mother know you are out?'[2] Primers on sociology often prove difficult books for students. The second reason for the gap which yawns between theoreticians – professional sociologists – and practitioners in society – parents, teachers, social and community workers of all kinds – is that there is as yet relatively little teaching of sociological understanding in our educational system.

For example, it is by no means unknown to find colleges of education which give no place to the subject in the preparation of teachers. This means that though a major part of their professional role is the understanding of people, inadequate attention is paid to the fact that people are subject to social pressures.

Currently then, there is a gap between the theoreticians – the professional and academic sociologists – and the practitioners[3] – the community workers in the widest meaning of the term, all those whose work demands primarily a skill in human relationships of various kinds. In the present context, this means that many of us are concerned with young people, work with them, seek to influence them, want to understand them but we often talk nonsense about young people. One reason is that our views have not been chastened by what careful enquiry and research has discovered about the rising generation.

The present volume aims to be a contribution to the bridging of this gap between theoretician and practitioner, between knowledge and responsibility: it may be said to have a practical aim in hoping to increase the information, insight and understanding of all those whose work as teachers, parents, youth and community workers, industrialists, planners, probation officers, personnel managers and child care officers brings them into close touch with young people. And we want to make it plain at the beginning that in referring to the 'young' we have actually in mind – not the fourteen- to twenty-year-olds of official youth service – but the more useful division of Abrams and others, that is fifteen to twenty-five if they are still unmarried.

Bruno Bettelheim has described the creative relationships between the younger and the older members of a community:[4]

Old age is happiest when it can take youth up to the threshold of the good and the new and, like the mythical father of the West, point out the Promised Land to its children, saying: you and only you in a hard fight will have to make this your own: because what is handed down to you, what you have not won for yourselves, is never truly your own.

Youth, on the other hand, is happiest when it feels it is fighting to reach goals that were conceived of but not realized by the generation before them. What the older generation then urgently wished for itself, but had to acknowledge as the hope of the future – this is the legacy of youth. That the preceding generation wished to create such a better world makes it a worthy standard for youth. To come closer to achieving it through its own efforts proves to youth that it is gaining its own rich maturity.

For only a fraction of this dream to come true we need an informed public opinion: this book wants to add a little to a wider and deeper social understanding of our young people.

Notes

1 J. B. Mays, 'Young people in contemporary society', p. 4, *Youth Service and Inter-professional Studies*, ed. in Bulman, Craft & Milson, Pergamon Press 1970.
2 Cf. C. Wright Mills, *The Sociological Imagination*, Penguin Books, p. 33ff., where the author reduces three unintelligible paragraphs of Talcott Parsons to two clear sentences.
3 Cf. *inter alia* the intriguing and amusing dedication to his wife of Talcott Parsons's *The Social System*, Routledge & Kegan Paul, 1952. 'To Helen, whose healthy and practical empiricism has long been an indispensable balance-wheel for an incurable theorist.'
4 Bruno Bettelheim, 'The problem of generations' in *Youth: Change and Challenge*, ed. by Erik H. Erikson, Basic Books, New York, 1963.

1 Youth in society

We begin by concentrating our attention upon particular young people. Some of the illustrations are fictional not documentary, but in a sense that does not matter, since novelists writing about adolescence are almost certain to a degree to be using their own experiences.

This method has two advantages. First, it serves to focus our observation upon the object of our quest for understanding – young people. Second, it is a dialectical device, used – as will later appear – to make a major point.

Stefan Zweig has given a graphic account of his own adolescence in Vienna during the early years of this century.[1] As a young teenager he belonged to a group of academically-gifted boys, whose thirst for intellectual and spiritual adventure was not slaked by what was served up to them at the Gymnasium. Their dissatisfaction and boredom grew because they lived where all the streams of European culture converged – in a city haunted by Haydn, Mozart, Beethoven, Schubert, Brahms and Johann Strauss. So they went through a period when it might be said that their education and personal development were interrupted by their schooling.[2]

> While the teacher delivered his time-worn lecture about the 'naïve and sentimental poetry' of Schiller, under our desks we read Nietzsche and Strindberg, whose names the good old man had never heard. A fever had come over us to know all, to be familiar with all that occurred in every field of art and science. In the afternoon we pushed our way among the university students to listen to the lectures, we visited all the art exhibitions, we went into the anatomy classrooms to watch dissections. We sniffed at all and everything with inquisitive nostrils. We crept into the rehearsals of the Philharmonic, we hunted about in the antique shops, we examined the booksellers' displays daily, so that we might know at once what had turned up since yesterday.

Recently two unconnected Jamaican families returned to the Caribbean island after nearly twenty years in Britain. They each took with them one adolescent child who had been born in Britain. The first, a boy, went to a Kingston school and suffered agonies of self-consciousness and shame because the other boys in the school mimicked his 'Brummie' accent. The second, a girl, went to a mountain village where householders are still carrying water and during her adolescent years she is experiencing culture shock.

In *Clayhanger* Arnold Bennett has drawn a convincing picture of Edwin, a young man struggling to free himself from the tight control of his father, Darius Clayhanger, and live his own life. He wants to be an architect, but the old man knows nothing of this ambition and assumes that his son will follow him in the printing business which he has laboriously built up. Edwin is too nervous to discuss the matter with his father and instead writes him a letter about his wishes. At the subsequent interview, Edwin is no match for the old man: it is all over in a few minutes and the ambition is gone for ever, 'sunk without trace'.

Richard Hughes in *High Wind in Jamaica* has a memorable passage describing the advent of self-consciousness which is a common feature of adolescence, for boys and girls alike.

> And then an event did occur to Emily, of considerable importance. She suddenly realized who she was . . . She had been playing house in a nook right in the bows, behind the windlass and, tiring of it, was walking rather aimlessly aft, thinking vaguely about some bees and a fairy queen, when suddenly it flashed into her mind that she was *she*. She stopped dead, and began looking all over her person which came within range of her eyes. She could not see much, except a fore-shortened view of the front of her frock, and her hands when she lifted them up for inspection: but it was enough for her to form a rough idea of the little body which she had suddenly realised to be hers. She began to laugh. 'Well,' she thought, in effect: 'Fancy you, of all people, going and getting caught like this. You can't get out of it now, not for a very long time, you'll have to go through with being a child, and growing up and getting old, before you'll be quit of this mad prank.'

And here, personally known to the writer, are three young people, in different parts of the world, working at their adolescent task in varying social and cultural circumstances.

A young man in Moscow confided in me. 'I have been brought up in an atheistic country to believe that there is no God. But sometimes, I think there might be one. Then I begin to feel guilty.'

In a hotel in Hong Kong, a fifteen-year-old girl works seven hours a day on the lift to earn the money for five hours a day secondary schooling. She takes her English books to work and studies them in the intervals of working the lift. She lives in a society where by tradition prestige is accorded the scholar, where parental and societal pressures are exerted upon young people to do well at school and have a white-collar job, but where educational provision is in short supply.

A young college student in Alabama told me of his intention to become a full-time worker for the integration of white and black people in the Deep South. But he had one psychological difficulty. Though his reason and his education told him that people of different coloured skins shared a common humanity, due to his upbringing, he could not repress an instinctive revulsion when he came into too close physical contact with a Negro. 'My mother always told me – Keep away from Black people: they are dirty and wicked.'

Thus we have a few pictures of young people chosen almost at random from hundreds of possibilities. If we were to ponder these tales, reflect upon their meaning in order to understand better what is happening, we could make one of two approaches (or we might, in fact, in the end, make both). We could stress the similarities in the experiences of these young people, pointing out the common elements: that in the main is the psychological approach. Or we could notice the differences in the experiences of these young people because they find themselves in varying social circumstances.

In the first, we might philosophize – and even rhapsodize thus – 'Ah youth! Reaching out to new experiences. Adolescence is a blossoming-time, a flowering period of the human spirit. Of course there are problems which arise from the heightened emotionality and the beckoning opportunities and the expanding horizons – so it is a time of stress and strain.'

And this is in fact how many writers have properly written about adolescence, though usually in less colourful terms than we have used. J. MacAlister Brew described the experience as a second birth. Here we are focusing attention on changes in the individual youngster – physical, physiological and psychological.

2

But a brief consideration of our examples shows that these young people were having different experiences because they were each in different social environments. Zweig's companions were compelled to develop their own peer resources in a cultural capital; the Jamaican youngsters were working out their adolescent task in a situation of culture conflict; Edwin Clayhanger lived in an industrial society where paternal authority was well established; Emily was part of an unusual background on any showing.

This brings us to make emphatically a point which is obvious enough, though often only half-acknowledged in thought and practice, and which is basic to our argument. It may be put in a number of ways. The society in which the adolescent has been brought up and lives, shapes the adolescent task. What he will feel guilty about, what he must strive for, what particular battles he may have to fight and win to achieve adulthood, what the symbols will be of achievement, status and acceptance, as well as the duration and intensity of the experience – all this comes from the community as well as from the individual and any universal aspects of the adolescent experience that there may happen to be. One of the accepted educational tags is, 'If you want to teach Johnny Latin, you must know Latin *and* Johnny': today, we ought to add, 'And a great deal about the society in which Johnny has grown up and the primary groups to which he has belonged.' Adolescence in fact is an experience at the meeting-place of physical, physiological and socio-cultural pressures – and we must not neglect the latter; it is a role-change as well as a rebirth; a grasp of the pressures which come from without are needed to understand the pressures from within. He is not only a 'new creature' with a different body and fresh desires, but he is, as it were, living in a 'new neighbourhood' where – to continue the figure – he doesn't yet know his neighbours, where the bus stop and post box are situated nor does he know just where the rut in the road is so that he can avoid it coming home late at night in the dark on his bike. To understand what is happening to the 'new creature' we must also scrutinize the 'neighbourhood'. This is what the Albemarle Report meant by saying that young people are the litmus paper of a society.

The point we are making, though an obvious one, may now be stated in longer form. In the life-cycle of the individual there is a period when he has ceased to be a child, but has not yet become an adult in the social and perhaps also in the biological sense. There are universal elements which characterize this time. In all societies there are physical and physiological changes leading to a new physical and significant experience: the search for adult identity and the playing of new social roles. For the rest, we have to take account of the fact that particular societies give their own shape to the adolescent task. And we have to study these particular societies if we want to understand the young people in them, and indeed, if we want to understand any one young person in them. We cannot know adolescents anywhere without a sustained effort to appreciate the social environment with which they are constantly and vitally interacting.

Is it possible to be any more exact? We think it is. Below are listed what we consider to be features of societies which are most likely to affect the adolescent experience.

1   What are the adult norms of behaviour? How are men and women expected to behave – in sex roles, in work roles, in family roles? If males, for example, are not accepted as adults until they have proved their physical courage, this will be part of the adolescent task for boys. Margaret Mead devoted a volume[3] to the study of the male and female roles in seven South Sea Island cultures and the related question of how boys and girls are socialized to play these roles. Among these small nations there are many variations in the expectations of male and female behaviour, and some of them sound strange to us. 'Here the Tchambuli women, brisk, unadorned, managing and industrious, fish and go to market: the men decorative and adorned, carve and paint and practise dance-steps, their head-hunting tradition replaced by the simple practice of buying victims to validate their manhood.'[4] And hence the adolescent task, the stage before adult status, differs in each of those societies. If ever we have a 'unisex' society – that is one where the distinctiveness of male and female roles has been seriously diminished – the experience of youth, for good or ill, will be transformed. We have chosen to concentrate here on sex roles. We could equally well have applied the argument to work or family roles. A youth, say, in Jamaica who can look forward to working on the land if he gets work at all and whom nobody will criticize if he begets several children before he marries, is living in a different world from a high school boy from a small American town,

of a Protestant family, who is looking forward to going to college.
2   What is perhaps even more decisive for the youngster is how firmly based is the normative structure of expected behaviour with which he is confronted. Is the society in which he is coming to manhood – and the adults who rule – supremely confident of their values and the whole cultural tradition which they wish to transmit? Then Johnny may have to stage a revolt in order to win his emotional spurs of maturity. Or is it a society which has been assailed by misgivings, anomic, pluralistic rather than monistic, which has lost confidence when speaking to its young, or which speaks with many voices? This society will present a different kind of challenge to Johnny. We leave this important subject now since it is the major preoccupation of our next chapter. It is our contention that the pace of social change is the main influence fashioning the adolescent task.
3   The wealth of a society is clearly another determinative influence upon the adolescent experience. Johnny and Mary may be living in a country where wholly inadequate resources are available for education and social welfare programmes, where only a favoured tiny minority go on to secondary education, where the drop-out in primary schools is high, where their adult prospects are limited, with the near certainty of marginal poverty and unemployment. On the other hand, Johnny and Mary may be members of a social group in a country where they can confidently look forward to going to college and have every encouragement and opportunity for the development of their gifts; and at the end of a long process of education, they know they will go into a society where their merits and efforts will earn economic rewards and psychological satisfactions. One marked difference is that in the second situation the period of adolescence tends to be extended: full adult status is usually delayed whilst there is economic dependence.[5]

If adolescence is to be seen against the backcloth of the culture in which it takes place, we may say then in general terms that it is the normative patterns, the stability and the wealth which we must identify in the backcloth.

The view that adolescence is a culturally conditioned experience receives confirmation when we consider the progress of the psychology of adolescence as an intellectual discipline.

During the modern period psychology has of course passed from the deductive approach to the inductive. This means that instead of philosophers reflecting in order to discover general principles which would explain human behaviour, men have looked at many examples of human behaviour and tried to detect in them any general principles. This, in ridiculous brevity, is what we mean by the 'scientific method'. But on the whole psychology was the last sphere in which it was applied. Man studied his physical environment in a detached way long before he began to take a careful look at himself. The method is now, however, well established in psychological enquiry. 'Grand theories' have given way to patient investigation: analysis and classification have taken the place of philosophizing, though obviously interpretation is still required. One indication is that it is no longer common to find in a university, that psychology is a branch of the faculty of philosophy.

The history of the 'scientific' study of the psychology of adolescence has followed this familiar course.[6] Ingenious theories mark the thinking of the Greeks and even the thinking of later philosophers like Rousseau. The writings of Stanley Hall are the beginnings of a new approach.[7]

[He] stands half-way between the philosophic fiction of past centuries and the controlled observation and experiment of the present. He was influenced by the nineteenth-century doctrine of evolution and he sought to transfer to the study of education the scientific exactness of the developing physical sciences. He explored children's minds and attitudes through the reminiscences which adults set down in response to his questionnaires and he analysed the self-expression of children through essays and directed questionnaires.

In other words, Hall tried to get at the facts.

His theoretical structure was taken over from Rousseau with due acknowledgment; he sees the child as repeating in himself the history of the race. 'The child comes from and harks back to a remoter past: the adolescent is neo-atavistic, and in him the later acquisitions of the race slowly become prepotent. Development is less gradual and more saltatory, suggestive of some ancient period of storm and stress when old moorings were broken and a higher level attained.'

'Storm and stress' might indeed be said to be the dominant

feature of Hall's picture of the adolescent. But this has not been confirmed by enquiries in other cultures about the experience of adolescence. For example, Margaret Mead describes the young people of New Guinea as not finding the years after puberty as a time of storm, stress or conflict; for girls they are a time of enforced passivity; for both sexes they represent the last years of liberty.[8]

In general it may be said that Hall fell a victim to the 'psychologist's fallacy'; he tended to assume that what he had found true of adolescents in one society was true of adolescents everywhere, as though there were a universal adolescent who could be measured in small town USA.[9] His conclusions are accompanied 'by the assumption (in spite of a careful collection of current anthropological evidence as to the difference of behaviour in different cultural settings) that this interpretation alone was true to the facts of human nature'.[10]

The subsequent history of the subject has been profoundly influenced by the social anthropologists[11] whose findings have demonstrated that what is expected of the adolescent will vary from culture to culture, and that adolescent behaviour and attitudes reflect these expectations. Perhaps nobody knows how far the influence of cultural environment can go, but its effect is considerable, reaching to the onset of puberty, says R. N. Franzblau. According to this research hundreds of Danish girls growing up in the United States reached puberty on an average six months earlier than Danish girls growing up in Denmark.[12]

The conclusion with which we began – that to understand teenage Johnny it is necessary to study Johnny's society – was the conclusion of the academic study of the psychology of adolescence. The pace with which this development took place is perhaps best illustrated by a quotation from a book on the subject written only a quarter of a century after the issue of Stanley Hall's massive tomes.

'Students of Stanley Hall will miss extensive reference to his voluminous pioneer works on adolescence. The fact is that methods of study and social conditions have been so modified within the twenty-five years just past, that such references would seem of historic value primarily, rather than of scientific or practical value today.'[13]

The most formidable presentation of the point, a classic work on the subject and an intellectual *tour de force*, is S. N. Eisenstadt's

From Generation to Generation.[14] The broad principle is stated on p. 21. 'At this point it is important for us to see that in every human society this biological process of transition through different age stages, the process of growing up and ageing, is subject to cultural definitions. It becomes a basis for defining human beings, for the informing of mutual relationships and activities, and for the differential allocation of rules.' Eisenstadt proceeds to apply this general consideration to adolescence in particular. He offers a hypothesis which may roughly be summarized as follows: Youth groups only develop in those societies where the family is inadequate for the socialization of young people. If Johnny and Mary can learn at home how to play all their social roles, they are unlikely to join youth groups.

Societies differ widely as to whether the norms of the family are close to the norms of the whole community: and this fact will affect the content of the adolescent experience.

It could be objected at this point that we are making heavy weather of two obvious propositions.

The first is that personality is a social product or, to put the matter colloquially, we are what we are because of the way we have been brought up – at a particular time in a particular nation. G. H. Mead has expounded this interpretation brilliantly.[15] The self is a looking-glass self. An individual only learns to think of himself as a 'self' because others treat him as such. Hence the elaborate games of 'let's pretend' that we play with babies and small children, pretending for example that they can understand words when in fact they cannot. We slowly learn to imagine how we appear to others and by adapting to ourselves the attitudes that others take to us, we learn to treat ourselves as objects as well as subjects. Without society there can be no self. 'The self, as that which can be object to itself, is essentially a social structure, and it arises in social experience.' The same truth has been expressed from the sociological point of view by C. Wright Mills:[16]

The sociological imagination enables its possessor to understand the larger historical scene in terms of its meaning for the inner life and the external career of a variety of individuals ... The first fruit of this imagination – and the first lessons of the social science that embodies it – is the idea that the individual can understand his own experience and gauge his fate only by becoming aware of those of all individuals in his circumstances.

It may be happily conceded that in this chapter we have done no more than give a particular application – in this instance, of adolescents – of the general proposition that the self is a social product to be understood in terms of social experiences. But it is maintained here that the exercise is justified and indeed necessary because it is the general proposition which is frequently overlooked or imperfectly grasped, at least, outside academic circles. When we begin the study of the social sciences – say psychology and sociology – most of us are capable of refusing to make any generalizations about any group of people, falling back on 'It all depends on the individual.' We may not at first be able to grasp that people are to be understood in terms of their similarities as well as their differences: that each individual, it is true, is unique but he is also moulded by social pressures from the secondary groups to which he belongs, like nation, class, city, trade union, and also the primary groups to which he belongs, like family and friendship groups.[17]

Perhaps the second objection is commoner and more formidable. In stressing the social determinants of the adolescence experience, have we not merely dwelt at length on a fact which is already universally recognized and acted upon? 'I suppose it's the way he's been brought up', people will say excusing a youthful misdemeanour. 'What else can you expect?' A more sophisticated comment might be, 'It is difficult for young people today growing up in a society which is confused about its values.' But it is our contention that this understanding at any depth is still unusual. Anybody who tries to say anything worth while about social groups of young people is likely to be met with the rejoinder, 'But that can't be true; our Johnny isn't like that.'

The reality of social and cultural pressures upon adolescents – and others – has not been integrated into our common ways of thinking and speaking. Even where it has been thus integrated there is often a need for us to be more specific and exact. Many who have responsibility for young people – parents, teachers, youth workers, personnel managers – are sometimes disposed, in commenting on adolescents, to make general statements like, 'He had a bad home.' This invites the immediate question, 'What kind of a bad home and how did it affect him?'

Notes

1 Stefan Zweig, *The World of Yesterday*, Cassell, 1953.
2 Ibid., pp. 40–1.
3 Margaret Mead, *Male and Female*, Penguin Books.
4 Ibid., p. 69.
5 This point is well brought out in Frank Musgrove's *Youth and the Social Order*, Routledge & Kegan Paul, 1964. In writing about young people in Britain during the Industrial Revolution, he shows that because they went to work at an earlier age, they reached social adulthood sooner than British youngsters in the 1960s. 'What shocked middle-class commentators on factory life in mid-Victorian England as much as the alleged immorality was the independence of the young' (p. 67).
6 Cf. 'Theories of Adolescence', chapter 14 of C. M. Fleming's *Adolescence: Its Social Psychology*, Routledge & Kegan Paul, 1963.
7 Fleming, ibid., p. 35
8 Margaret Mead, *Growing up in New Guinea*, Penguin Books.
9 Though it is only fair to add that in his second volume he has a chapter on comparative anthropology and he devotes some attention to the study of American society. Dr C. M. Fleming thinks he also underestimates individual variations among adolescents as well as cultural.
10 C. M. Fleming, op. cit., p. 38. For a short useful summary of the history of the psychology of adolescence, cf. chapter 1 of James Hemming's *Problems of Adolescent Girls*, Heinemann, 1967.
11 Most influential among these writers have, of course, been Ruth Benedict, *Patterns of Culture*, Routledge & Kegan Paul, 1935, and Margaret Mead.
12 R. N. Franzblau, 'Race differences in mental and physical traits', *Archives Psychology*, No. 177, 1935.
13 L. Hollingworth, *The Psychology of the Adolescent*, A. and C. Black, 1930.
14 Collier-Macmillan, 1964.
15 In *Mind, Self and Society*, University of Chicago Press, 1934.
16 *The Sociological Imagination*, Penguin Books, pp. 11, 12.
17 Yet one of the most frequent quotations of our time is John Donne's 'No man is an *Island*, entire of it self.' Is this an inarticulate recognition of the social content of our experience?

Suggestions for further reading

Fictional accounts of adolescence

Barstow, Stan, *A Kind of Loving*, Penguin Books.
McInnes, Colin, *Absolute Beginners*, Penguin Books.
Moravia, Alberto, *Two Adolescents*, Penguin Books.
Salinger, J. D., *Catcher in the Rye*, Penguin Books.
Sillitoe, Alan, *Saturday Night and Sunday Morning*, W. H. Allen, 1958.
Sillitoe, Alan, *The Loneliness of the Long-Distance Runner*, W. H. Allen, 1959.

Autobiographical and biographical accounts of adolescence

Bethge, Eberhard, *Dietrich Bonhoeffer. A Biography*, Collins, 1970, chapter 1.
Chaplin, Charles, *My Autobiography*, Penguin Books, chapter 6.
Gosse, Edmund, *Father and Son*, Heinemann, 1964.
McCarthy, Mary, *Memories of a Catholic Childhood*, Penguin Books.
Ironmonger, F. A., *William Temple, Archbishop of Canterbury*, Oxford University Press, 1948, chapters 1–3.
Maxwell, Gavin, *The House of Elrig*, Longmans, 1965.
Russell, Bertrand, *Autobiography 1872–1914*, Allen & Unwin, 1967–8, vol. 1, chapter 2.
Wilson, Angus, *The World of Charles Dickens*, Secker & Warburg, 1970, chapter 2.

On the general theme that personality is a social product

Berger, Peter, *Invitation to Sociology*, Penguin Books.
Cotgrove, Stephen, *The Science of Society*, Allen & Unwin, 1967, chapter 1.
Davis, Kingsley, *Human Society*, MacMillan, 1948, part 2.
Worsley, Peter, *Introducing Sociology*, Penguin Books, chapter 1.

On the theme that adolescence is to be studied where it takes place

Erikson, Erik H. (ed.), *Youth: Change and Challenge*, Basic Books, 1963.
Mays, J. B., *The Young Pretenders*, Michael Joseph, 1965, chapters 1–3.
Smith, Cyril, *Adolescence*, Longmans, 1968.
Wilson, Bryan, *The Youth Culture and the Universities*, Faber, 1970, chapters 1, 6, 9.

2 Youth at a time of rapid social change

Social change

Social change is a matter of common observation and personal experience. Among many inhabitants of the earth, it is a frequent topic of conversation.

We may find it in the reminiscences of older people. 'I can remember the time when . . .' they may say to an audience of younger contemporaries, who may be attentive and wide-eyed if they have not heard the story too often before. In truth the memory of an old man may well span an interval which covers many social changes. Perhaps he can remember the time when the first electric tramways were operated.[1] The sprawling housing estate which contains its third generation is perhaps built where, as a boy, he journeyed for a walk in the country. He can remember the first motor-car, the first cinema, the first radio programme, and, of course, the first television programme. But his memory stores other changes and not all of them aspects of the physical culture which we have inherited, but changes which are more directly and intimately concerned with the style of living and the forms of interaction and communication of the people in these islands.

Perhaps he can remember when women's clothing covered more of their bodies than is the common usage of today; when there were few educational opportunities for poor boys however clever they might be; when the community offered little organized caring for the underprivileged, handicapped and old; when inequalities between members of different social classes were approved, recognized and organized into appropriate patterns of behaviour;[2] and when relatively large numbers of people were born, lived and died in the same community.

The reality of social change may be brought home to us in several ways. We may watch an old film and not fail to notice how much is different from less than fifty years ago – styles of dress, means of transport, fashion of humour, design of buildings and pattern of human relationships in home, at work, and in the street. Or we may visit a town or city where we lived many years ago and observe the sum of the changes.[3]

Sociologists have been concerned to think about social change in a disciplined way, collecting facts, analysing and suggesting

theoretical concepts as is their wont.[4] With some of their speculations we are here only marginally concerned; the following five
areas of sociological enquiry move in a mounting scale of importance for our purpose:

1   Direction. In the days when the theory of evolution had cap-
tured the imagination of educated people, it was tempting to
assume that human societies were subject, like biological species,
to the process of natural selection; and it was an easy transition to
the belief in the inevitable progress of human societies. Sufficient
here to say that this view has been widely abandoned. It is a vast
over-simplification: a belief in the inevitability of the progress of
human societies does justice neither to the grim facts of human
history, nor to the complexities of the issue involved in social
change.[5] Cultural progress is not to be confused with man's growing mastery over the forces of nature. If there is moral progress on
the whole, it can only be expressed in the general terms which
Ginsberg used in his Fraser lecture:

a   A tendency to universalism, a consideration of others outside
the narrow confines of the tribe.
b   A tendency towards regarding morality, not merely as pru-
dential, but as a pursuit of virtue for its own sake.
c   A tendency for the moral judgment to become more sophisticated – to ask, say, not merely 'what did this man do?' but
'why did he do it?'

2   Source. What is it that causes social change? The obvious
answer is 'inventions which lead to technological changes'. We
have only to think for a moment of the impact at various times
upon the British people of the advent of the steam-engine, the
bicycle, the motor-car, the aeroplane, the radio and the television,
to see how true this is. But sociologists would want to insist – and
presumably not only because it is their vested interest – that there
are social and cultural determinants of change as well as technological. There is in fact cultural conditioning of technological
advance: this is partly what we mean by the common saying,
'necessity is the mother of invention'. Ideas are put forward and
machines are invented often because a situation of stress, danger,
threat, loss, pain or inconvenience demands them. Obvious illustrations abound. The safety-belt came for cars because of society's
reactions to the appalling toll in road accidents. When it was

necessary to dispel fog over airports, twenty-five different ways of doing it were put forward. More than this, there are cultural factors which can in general terms encourage social change. One is the diffusion of knowledge. Many African peoples, for example, have been profoundly affected by the introduction of Western technology – in the view of some observers, they have been affected disastrously since old established ways of community living have been seriously damaged. Equally, it is true that resistance to change may come from cultural factors. The exploiting of many inventions has been impeded and truth suppressed. There was opposition in the early days to the use of contrivances so diverse as umbrellas, contraceptives, railways and motor-cars.

Nor is it true that technological advances are always the prime source of change. In other words, social and cultural factors sometimes operate to effect change in a direct way and do not always need to express themselves through technology. Social values, ideologies, wars, strains and stresses and charismatic leaders all play their part at various times and to varying degrees.

This is not to seek to deny the major role in social change which is played by technological advances.[6] But as with other subjects we tend to over-simplify the issue: we find refuge in one easily-grasped principle and are blind to other considerations and modifications: we are seized by the sight of the great pearl and have no eyes for the lesser pearls. All that we are concerned to say here is that the technological changes are not the only source of change and that even technological changes are not wrought in isolation from the total community by bright individuals who have brilliant ideas.

We now move to a consideration of factors in social change with which our general subject is more closely involved.

3 When we talk about 'social change', what we often mean, more accurately, is 'cultural change': in other words we are not confining our attention only to changes in structure and function, social organization. We mean changes that may occur in any one or more parts of the total way of life in the society with which we are concerned. This may include family, religion, art, transport and leisure habits.

And this of course is what we find: profound changes in any part affect the whole. The motor-car has been responsible for a new important industry but it has also changed the habits and increased the mobility of millions of people; it has given rise to new norms of behaviour about not driving carelessly or even tolerating a noisy exhaust. Most important, changes cannot be isolated to one segment of a community.[7] The introduction of a new factory into a rural community may as they say 'change the character of the place'. Once in a remote Yorkshire coastal fishing village, I was struck by the urbanized habits of the local residents and by the obvious decay of the traditional style of life. But an old man there told me that in the First World War, there were young men who had never left the village until they left it to join the Army and fight in Flanders. The internal combustion engine shattered the isolation and changed much else beside. A traditional American saying runs, 'If a man makes a better mousetrap the world will make a beaten path to his door.' But if we are to take that with absurd literalism, there is more involved than the building of a flourishing business and the making of a private fortune. As the customers rush forward they will jostle each other and grow angry or laugh, make friends or enemies, form alliances and enter into agreements: new forms of interaction will emerge and new patterns of relationships be formed. The Industrial Revolution in Britain, for example, made so much difference to the British family that social histories are prone to regard it as the dividing line in their records. The point here is that what we usually mean by the term 'social change' can have very wide implications for the lives of people.

4   Change is a widespread phenomenon in human societies. Many of us are in the habit of dividing human societies into 'changing' and 'unchanging'. This procedure – reminiscent of the convenient 'goodies and baddies' structure of the Westerns – is one further example of the temptation to over-simplification in thinking about human societies which we have already noticed. We must surrender the stereotype that historical and primitive societies are unchanging by complete contrast with modern societies. It is logical to suppose that there is some change going on in all human societies. For one thing, the present members are growing older and new members are being born. And as men live with each other, they affect the behaviour of others. This seems at least a reasonable assumption in a human society where the membership is composed of men and women who are not entirely puppets on strings.

5   So it follows that if we want to gain a little more understanding of any human society the question to ask is not about the fact, but about the pace of social change. All times may be times of change, but some are times of rapid social change – and the latter is clearly more serious and far-reaching in its effects.

In 1906 a book was written about a 'primitive' people, the Todas of India. The appendix contains a reference to a book about the same people written three hundred years before by a Portuguese missionary. When the two works are compared it is clear that the several centuries have seen no profound changes in the way of life of these people. Change may be there but in relation to the whole community it is so slow as to be almost imperceptible. The contrast with a modern industrialized society makes the difference almost one of kind rather than degree. A British boy of thirteen may well have seen as many changes in the outline of the city where he lives as his grandfather has seen. Big changes take place in a lifetime and often in a decade. The norm of British middle-class wives going out to work – a development that represents a significant variation of traditional patterns of class behaviour – was fully formed in the fifteen years after the war. So rapid are some of the changes in a country like ours, that one difficulty of government is that our rulers cannot always be sure what is happening: statistics are rapidly out of date and trends are reversed. The Lord Mayor's parlour in Birmingham has on the wall a picture of the view of the city from the site 150 years ago. Visitors often express astonishment at the changes – green fields are displayed on the old print. What those visitors may not realize is that there have been even bigger alterations to the structure and contours of the city centre in the last ten years. Whole streets have a way of disappearing apparently overnight! Technology is, of course, the main agent of rapid social change.[8] Cultural forces not linked with inventions work more slowly. We may in fact say that in countries strongly affected by modern technology, there is an accelerated rate of social change, a chain reaction of adjustments. 'The differences between the America of 1950 and that of 1960 are greater than those between 1900 and 1910: because of the accelerating rate of innovations, more things change, and more rapidly in each successive generation. As a result, the past grows progressively more different from the present in fact, and seems more remote and irrelevant psychologically.[9]

Rapid change has a bigger effect

Rapid and extensive social change clearly makes more demand on people than gradual change or change in only part of their social experience. We have seen that rapidity of change and extensiveness often exist together: individuals living in advanced societies today might be forgiven for wishing that 'not everything would change so quickly'. They may pine for enough time to make the adjustments gradually, to 'play themselves in', to use a cricketing term. A man who has to learn new techniques at work returns home to find that his wife has different ideas of her role and that he cannot understand his teenage children. Meanwhile, the local cinema has closed. Some of the stress and strain of modern living for middle-aged and elderly people arises from this feeling of 'not knowing where they are': the old familiar landmarks have been removed.

At such times – and as part of the chain reaction to which reference has already been made – change becomes a fashion: because so much is changing, people begin to wonder why everything should not change. This is illustrated in the probably apocryphal story of the dealer who advertised, 'We have the latest in antiques.' The process may go so far that a whole generation may see themselves as strikingly distinctive from what has gone before and may even seek to encourage a new title for themselves like the 'New Elizabethans'. This is not to enter into any value-judgments about change versus stability. If there are generations attracted to what is new simply because it is new, who are thereby disposed to give no careful scrutiny to the old, established and traditional realities, it could equally well be argued that there is an unhelpful and ingrained conservatism in many communities and that 'frontier societies' exhibit energy and hope. It is not the present purpose to pursue this argument. Rather we are concerned to describe part of the psychological atmosphere for individuals who live at times of rapid social change. One does not hear today a statement which had a vogue at one time – 'If it is not necessary to change, it is necessary not to change.' If the 'silent majority' are conservatively inclined as we are often told, many of them are likely to keep quiet about it out of deference to the popular drift of opinion: we are reluctant to announce ourselves as 'squares' or 'fuddy-duddies' – and the growth of colloquial terms to describe old-fashioned attitudes is significant.

By contrast a statement like that of Bertrand Russell – 'Those who feel certainty are stupid: those with imagination are full of doubt' – gains growing acceptance at a time like this.

The experience of adjustment contains several distinct but related parts. Some of these are:

1   There is the adjustment to new physical realities. We have 'to learn to live with' – and the frequent phrase is again significant – the jumbo jet plane, the motor-car and the noisy transistor radio. Statesmen can be rushed to any part of the world in a few hours but perhaps their lives are more fretful and stressful than their predecessors', in consequence. Daily driving in a city during the rush hours is another example. Soccer is changing its character because speed of travel makes international games possible. One wonders if the day will come when only a few top teams will be watched on television with a live audience on the ground paid to create the right noises of crowd responses. Local choirs and dramatic societies and operatic companies find it harder to gather an audience because of the competition of the mass-media. The moon does not seem as remote since millions of viewers saw men landing on it. Some of the new devices create stress and anxiety; some of them undoubtedly threaten liberty like the many devices for listening in to private conversations. But the present intention is not to suggest that the physical realities of our time are always a threat; it would be ludicrous to deny that they often enrich our lives and broaden our experience. The point here is that they are a 'new' part of our environment to which we have to adjust.

2   There are new rules to be learned: new situations arise for which there are no precedents. Much of human behaviour is socially-defined: we follow the normative patterns that have grown up in our society usually without thinking about it; anything else would be intolerable since it would mean that we should have to stop and think out every situation for ourselves; we want to behave usually in socially-acceptable ways that, far from giving offence, will win the approval of others. Even when there is a dilemma because we are confronted with a situation which is new to us, we are usually content to say, 'What do people usually do?'[10] This is what sends people out buying little books on the etiquette of marriage when a family wedding is planned; it explains many conversations with our friends when we seek advice on several lines of action. Behind the norms of daily behaviour, beyond the

3

social definitions of individual action, usually lie long traditions. It is easy to see how this applies not only to marriage customs but to parent–child relationships, courting customs and how people generally should treat each other across the divisions of age and sex. Folk sayings of a bygone age expressed the norms of acceptable behaviour. 'A woman's place is in the home'; 'Children should be seen and not heard.' But what we are noticing here is that rapid social change creates situations which are new and for which there are no traditional norms. Incidentally, this is why moral systems from a previous age are found to be inadequate and absurd if they are interpreted in a literal and rigid way, though it may be argued that if they are offered as general principles, their validity has better voice. 'Thou shalt love thy neighbour as thyself' may be capable of an interpretation in any conceivable kind of human situation. But narrower interpretations are entangled in unconvincing casuistry because the circumstances which have arisen were never envisaged.[11] How many children shall we have? Do we send Johnny to the comprehensive or the grammar school? Do we disown Tom because he is 'hooked on cannabis'? Do we turn Mary out of the house because she admits to having sexual intercourse with her boy friend – and 'there is no risk of a baby'? How do we decide financial priorities between a holiday overseas, a new car, colour television and looking after 'the old folk'?

In society as a whole, it also appears that 'new occasions teach new duties': we are presented with choices for which there are no historical precedents. How much support ought we to give to transplant operations? How much of our resources ought to be devoted to keeping old people alive longer? Already there is a 'cultural euthanasia' simply because there is only a thin line dividing the act of killing people and trying not too strenuously to keep them alive. With a growing and ageing population, the time of death may in the future be more directly a personal and social choice.

New rules are needed for unprecedented situations: we are confronted with daily choices for which there are no long-established usages. In several of the illustrations mentioned above, no choice was possible in former times since individuals and societies had to take what 'Fate' did to them. Technical advance has put more power into the hands of men. In other cases, changed conditions have created new circumstances. To use a trite instance –

there is no ancient moral code, nor could there be, which says, 'When thou sittest in thy garden on a Sabbath afternoon, thou shalt turn down the volume on thy radio' or 'Thou shalt have no noisy exhaust on thy motor-car.'

3   It follows that there are new roles to be learned at a time of rapid social change. Society is a place where there are norms, that is socially-acceptable ways of behaving in given situations to which most of us usually conform. But norms relate to another socio-logical definition – roles and status.[12] What is socially acceptable behaviour varies between different people according to the rela-tionship they have. 'Don't speak to your father like that' is a recognition of the reality which can often be heard in family life. A man has sexual expectations of his wife which he cannot reason-ably entertain of other women. Much of our daily behaviour is structured by what we know is expected of us. Thus, we are un-likely to swear in the presence of the vicar, or if we do, we shall hastily apologize. Only a minority of the citizens of this country will detain the milkman on the step with religious talk or issue an invitation to prayer. Equally we shall not look for 'old heads on young shoulders'.

From one point of view, a human society is a place where the individual members are each occupying a number of statuses and fulfilling a number of roles. And these usually relate to occupation, age, sex and kin. In stable times everybody 'knows where he is' in relation to other people. There is a clear consensus, which has been handed down as part of one's cultural inheritance, as to how one ought to behave in different kinds of relationships. And where doubts arose there were always clues, often indeed symbols of social position. People high up the scale, with a better education, spoke with a different accent and wore better, smarter clothes. One could not mistake the sex even of an effeminate man since he wore the clothes and had the hair style of a male. On the whole, people looked their age. It is not nearly so simple and straightforward at a time of rapid social change: not merely in the confusion of sym-bols.[13] New roles are emerging. Traffic wardens, for example, have low prestige with much power. How does one approach them? Like the headmaster or the school caretaker? What kind of bearing does one adopt towards the civil servant who comes to enquire whether or not you are paying S.E.T. contributions on your domestic help? Again there has been juxtaposition in the prestige accorded to varying occupations. Bank clerks and teachers have slipped a rung or two down the ladder and skilled craftsmen have climbed higher.

A more frequent cause of confusion however is the new interpretations which are given to old roles. In many families, the old-type father who ruled 'with a rod of iron' has given way to the father who is troubled by what he has heard about allowing his children to develop their own personalities, and their requiring understanding and tolerance. Where, and in so far as this has happened, the role of father has to a degree been redefined. There are many more examples. Teachers, we are told, must abandon their old authority; they must teach children rather than subjects; nay, rather, they must learn with the children rather than teach them; and they must have skill in social and community work. The role and status of the teacher is in process of redefinition. Observers insist that policemen must become community workers as well as law enforcement officers. Leading industrialists, we are told, must learn to live with industrial democracy.

4   Finally, there is an adjustment to be made which in a sense is inclusive of the three which have gone before: social changes alter the values of a society and rapid social change alters them rapidly. Again one can hear echoes of this in the remarks of old people. 'Children daren't behave like that in my young days.' 'People knew their place when I was a lad.' 'I don't know what things are coming to.' Due allowance may be made for nostalgia, for faulty memories, for the fact that distance lends enchantment to the view, that a certain English verb might run, 'I reminisce: thou exaggeratest: he lies'. But usually what is left is the recognition of a basic shift of values in the community.

One generation is obviously linked to another by cultural tradition. Societies contain elements of stability as well as change. Complete discontinuity between generations would be impossible and it is instructive to find that even those countries which delight to proclaim themselves as revolutionary do not succeed in fact in making a complete break with the past: national characteristics have a way of reasserting themselves. Modern Russia under the Communists is curiously like the Russians under the Tsars, having, for example, the same stress upon the corporate personality of 'Mother Russia'. Perhaps this has become more explicit in recent times. The emphasis upon Russia's past – as seen for example in the careful preservation of historic churches as museums – is part of the evidence. In the Peter-Paul Fortress in Leningrad a statue of Peter the Great is accorded an honoured place. How can Communists revere the memory of a Tsar? It is carefully explained to the enquiring visitor that though he was the Tsar, he had also made himself the master of fourteen trades. Germany, defeated in the Second World War, and prompted by the victorious Allies, renounced its Nazi past and embraced democracy; but the new era did not eradicate the elements in the German character which made Hitler possible – and elements which admittedly can be put to better use – like love of order, acceptance of authority and industriousness.

Thus one generation is bound to another: there is a communication of norms and the values which lie behind norms. To parody Donne, 'no generation is an Island, entire of itself'. If this were not so there could be no socialization process since this presumes that newcomers to a society – whether born into it or migrating into it – are to be persuaded to accept an inherited way of living. But the links between generations are patently not equally strong. In some ages men are found stressing stability and authority; in others, their attention is caught by new ways and the discontinuities.

Social change in general, and rapid social change in particular, not only presents men with new physical realities, with which they have to cope, and points to the necessity for new rules and new roles, but it alters some of the basic value assumptions on which men live together. In our own time and country, we can see what the effect of the 'anti-baby' pill is having on sexual ethics and the sexual relationships of men and women generally. We can see how the status of women is changing because they are gradually narrowing the gap educationally and occupationally with men. We can see that the norm of the authority of fathers has been affected because the majority of married women go out to work and many children have a better education and better prospects than their fathers.

'Anomie' is a word which has been used with slightly varying meanings by different sociologists. It cannot mean the collapse of any consensus of values in a human society; it is hard to see in that case how the human association could continue.[14] 'Anomie' more generally and realistically refers to an erosion of accepted values, but, though never complete, this erosion can go a long way and reveal marked contrasts between the experience of living in one generation and another. Perhaps looking back we exaggerate the stability, cohesiveness and solidarity of those ages which we like to think of as 'quiet', but the evidence suggests that they were not subject to the constant shaking of the foundations which is a feature of many modern societies.

> Almost any kind of behaviour will be championed as right, or at least not wrong, by some groups or factions in society. On the morality of hardly any issue is there widespread agreement. Within the last two decades even the law, usually slow to reflect changes in moral attitudes, has been changed on capital punishment, corporal punishment, obscenity, betting and prostitution, and very nearly changed on homosexuality.[15]

No elaborate arguments are required to demonstrate that the experience of the individual is profoundly affected by a state of 'anomie' in his society, though of course, he may not be articulate about the effects nor indeed realize what is happening to him. It was once written of a French monarch that he would have been all right in quiet times, but unfortunately he inherited a revolution. Chinoy points to the extreme results of these stresses and demands:[16]

> The anomie stemming from these trends gives rise to extensive personal breakdown – suicide and mental illness – and to various forms of deviant behaviour such as crime, delinquency, bohemianism, and other eccentricities. It also stimulates totalitarian political movements that offer to solve pressing economic and political problems and to restore meaning, stability and security – albeit at a price.

But for the sake of our argument, we may content ourselves with less extreme effects. The citizen of a country of anomie may feel:

a That for his own behaviour, he is thrown more on his own resources and decisions: less of what he does is socially-defined. Of course, there are those for whom this will represent liberty. But others will feel the lack of support from group and community norms. There is an inevitable confusion which arises when the moral is not commonly the conventional. In this connection – though it is to anticipate the application of the point which is pursued in the next section – we may note an oft-quoted passage from J. B. Mays on the experience of adolescents in British society:[17]

One of the many social factors which may predispose
adolescents in our society to anxiety, doubt and indecision
was long ago mentioned by Margaret Mead. It consists in
the amazing number of choices presented to them, as on the
threshold of maturity, they begin to assume responsibility for
more and more areas of their own lives. The world at this
stage of the youngsters' development looks more like a
gigantic cafeteria or a vast emporium than anything else. The
only difference perhaps is that there are no obvious price
labels attached to the varying choices so temptingly
arranged.

b That experience has less authority. The most serious consequence is that older people – whether they are parents, teachers, workers, or merely senior citizens – are listened to with less patience. For a new situation, their longer time on earth is counted as irrelevant. In extreme cases, this tendency grows into what can be described as a 'cult of youth'.

c That many forms of social control are losing their power. Conformity obviously depends upon consensus. Law and order can never depend alone on the number of policemen, since in that case there would never be enough policemen to go round. It relies on respect for law and order, on the laws not being too far removed from the norms, the accepted standards. Many of the informal agencies of social control are established traditional aspects of authority – churches, schools, family. These are precisely the agencies which are undermined in situations of anomie.

d That the agents of socialization and education in a society do not speak with the same voice. The school, for example, becomes isolated from the rest of society; it may offer a value-system which is contradicted by what happens in the homes of many scholars and in the community at large. Police can no longer always rely on public support and sympathy in the enforcement of the law. The churches cease to be broadly representative of the population and become minority groups with a rare ideology. The Church of England looks less and less like the Church in England.

The fragmentation of the socializing agencies at a time of rapid social change may be an emotional matter for many ordinary citizens though they may not be able to put it into words.

Adolescents are among those who are most affected by social change

Not everybody is equally affected by rapid social change. For example, traditional patterns of community living, 'the old ways', tend to persist in rural districts: they are relatively isolated from 'where it is happening': change takes place more slowly since private behaviour comes under closer public scrutiny. Even a small country like Britain has areas which are comparatively isolated and where social habits have not changed to anything like the extent that they have in major cities. Likewise, on the long train journey from Moscow to Leningrad the traveller glancing out of the window may see groups of people (gathered at crossings) that, judging from their dress and demeanour, he may think to have strayed from the nineteenth century. Conversely, there are those who are the pioneers of new styles of living in days of rapid social change. Among these we should place the intellectual *élite* who have the ability and the confidence to think things through for themselves. Bertrand Russell's autobiographies introduce us to some nineteenth-century people in this country who were unashamedly living by the standards of twentieth-century 'permissive' Britain.[18] 'The groups most affected are usually in elite or vanguard positions: those in roles of intellectual leadership usually initiate innovations and make the first psychological adaptions to them, integrating novelty with older values and institutions and providing in their persons models which exemplify techniques of adaptions to the new social order.'[19]

Similarly, rapid social change has varying effects on different age-groups. It does not present young children with agonizing choices and old people, long established in their own style of living, may know only marginal stress. Among those most affected are youths in the process of making a commitment to the future.

The young, who have outlived the social definitions of
childhood and are not yet fully located in the world of adult
commitments and roles are most immediately torn between
the pulls of the past and the future. Reared by elders who
were formed in a previous version of the society, and
anticipating a life in a still different society, they must
somehow choose between the competing versions of past
and present.[20]

Readers of the literature on the psychology of adolescence are
familiar with the illustration which is used time and again to illustrate the point. In historical and primitive societies there are
usually initiation rites or rites of passage which mark the youngsters' unambiguous attainment of adult status. They often test his
knowledge of community laws and his rights and duties and his
ability to bear pain or display courage. The ritual may be related
to work, sex, fighting and general community roles. It provides a
social occasion – saying to the assembled onlookers, 'He is an adult
now: treat him as one'; and a private experience – saying to the
individual youngster, 'you are an adult now: behave as one'.

By contrast, in modern societies there only remain wan vestiges
of the precise definition of adulthood, and these are usually little
more than symbolic remnants, like the birthday card with the
embossed key, or are associated with minority ethical or religious
groups, like bar mitzvahs. And like relics they serve to remind us
of a vanished age and call our attention to the peculiarities for
young people of an age like the present where there are unusual
breaks in cultural continuity, lack of clear social goals and gaps in
the communication links across the generations.

The young growing up in Britain or any other Western country
inherit a chaos of disordered values. Present confusion about
moral standards and the changing climate of opinion on what is
right and wrong is well explored in the Eppel's account of their
enquiry into the ethical views of adolescents.[21] Let us take one
illustration only, where it is perhaps necessary to say that we seek
here to be non-judgmental, which is the intention of this total
argument. We are trying to describe a situation of 'anomie' – remarkable enough in itself – not seeking to make a judgment on
who is right and wrong. At a meeting of teachers in July 1963
Dr Henderson said, 'I don't myself consider that the young men

and women who plan to marry and who have sexual intercourse before they marry are unchaste. I simply can't convince myself that they are immoral.' Adults of no less authority expressed strong disagreement. Truly, young people in Britain today, unlike most of their historical predecessors, are no longer presented with a fairly solid block of societal and adult unanimity about what is right in important areas of their experience. Nor should one suppose, of course, that this is only true for sex ethics: it extends to most areas of belief and behaviour.

In the last section, we noted that rapid change affects the rules, roles and values of a society. It is easy to see how this makes a special impact on adolescents. Societies of consensus – that is where the inherited value and normative systems are not seriously questioned – do not in fact emphasize age as a principle of social differentials:[22] and such countries are not notable for the development of a 'youth subculture'. One can still see traces of this phenomenon where a 'persecuted minority' struggle for their rights. Welsh nationalism, for example, draws together all age groups. The results of pluralism can be viewed in two quarters. First, we can ask what are the frequent effects on young people themselves; and second, how do they affect the approaches which the adult population make to the young.

Observers have not been slow to point out that one difficulty of growing up in a developed country is that there may be nothing to rebel against: in many other ages the young have won their emotional spurs by staging a revolt against adult authority. Innumerable hortatory and emotional speeches have been given on this theme. It has been pointed out that 'we have been able to give the rising generation everything except a faith to live by'; they have secured many material privileges; they are taller, fatter, healthier and have more money and privileges and prospects than any previous generation of teenagers; but 'all the old signposts have been removed'.

But when full allowance has been made for the value-loaded content of these utterances, there remains an element which corresponds to something real in the experience of youngsters growing up in say West Germany, the USA. or Britain. It has been pointed out that many of the heroes of modern films and plays have no fathers, or fathers who are inadequate or psychologically absent. 'If only just once, they would tell me what *they* think I should do', moaned an American son. What is not there to rebel against may also be felt as a lack of support. Not every youngster, by any means, wants to be an innovator. Others may feel there is an adult world of values, but it is inadequate, materialistic, 'plastic', hypocritical, part of a 'rat-race'. Even the sober Albemarle Report[23] slipped in one explosive sentence, 'There does not seem to be at the heart of society a courageous and exciting struggle for a particular moral and spiritual life – only a passive, neutral commitment to things as they are.'

Adolescents today receive fewer specified definitions from their society. In their idealism particularly, they may feel isolated and alienated. Though some of the consequences may work out well, they can be less secure. We examine these effects later in the light of the adolescent task.

Similarly, the cultural discontinuities associated with rapid change press upon adults as they approach young people and try to build relationships with them. They share with the adolescents their own confusion about the social role of the adolescent and often indeed approach them as 'marginal people'. Who are these creatures who perhaps have left school but are not socially recognized adults, whom everybody says inhabit a world that is unexplored territory for adults? True, they have recently been granted adult majority at eighteen, but this is probably mostly due to their own pressures and threats. We continue to give them socially and psychologically a graded and delayed acceptance of their adulthood. Adults can no longer assume that they know everything that the youngster needs to know in order to be fitted for adult life. Hence in many places there has been an unusual strain on old-young relationships and some widening of the generation gap.

Adolescents need adults no less than young children need them, though they want a different relationship with them. Yet there are indications that communications between adolescents and adults have deteriorated and that we are witnessing more than the historic tensions between the generations. Young people often feel that they cannot talk over with parents the things that are worrying them. 'They would not understand.' The main reasons for this appear to lie not with any moral deterioration, as it is the fashion of some to proclaim, but rather in profound changes in the organized life of the community. Industrialization renders the home less able to prepare the youngster for all of his life in society; he has, for example, to learn specialized work roles outside the home. More technological change further widens the gap by creating yet other 'worlds' which are not directly influenced by the home, for example, the 'world' of entertainment.

There has been a loss of adult confidence with the young in many quarters, and this was only to be expected. The Albemarle Report had a perceptive chapter called 'Young People To-day'. Ten years later – such is the pace of present change – it is seriously out of date as a statement on the sociology of British youth. There is nothing there, for example, about drug-taking, the challenge of a multi-racial society, the changing age of social majority or students' protest movements or demands for participation.

One view, significantly, has gained widespread interest. Matza holds that there is a subterranean conversation between teenage rebellion and deviance on the one hand and conventional standards on the other, and that through this contact both are modified.[24]

This section then has concerned itself with the fact that adolescents are among the most vulnerable members of the community to the effects of rapid social change. They are unusual – though they may not be unique – in finding that their society often fails to offer them clear guidance about important matters, not least their own role and status. Though this failure may be linked with youthful confusion, alienation and delinquency, we are far from saying that it is necessarily always and wholly bad. Confronted with a stark choice between dangerous freedom and comfortable security, there are a few at least who will choose the former. Nor are we saying that there is a magic wand which can be waved to transform the contemporary scene. It is unthinkable, for example, that any leader in a Western democracy could advocate visual symbols for adulthood – say beards for boys at nineteen and mini-skirts for girls at eighteen. We are content to try to describe as accurately as possible, though at present in the broadest sociological terms, the experience of being young at a time of rapid social change.

There are several ways in which we might summarize our present contention. One is by means of a table – useful but over-simplified – contrasting the relevant features in stable and changing societies. It deals, of course, with trends rather than hard opposing totalities.

Stable	*Changing*
General agreement on what is right and good and enjoyable (firm normative structure).	Many disagreements on what is right and good and enjoyable (changing normative structure).
Most people 'know their place' and stay in it most of their lives: static society (clear role structure).	Much questioning about how people should behave towards each other in different relationships: many changes for individuals socially and geographically (role ambiguity and social and geographical mobility).
Older people – parents, teachers, parsons – have authority which comes from their longer experience.	Authority of older people undermined: their experience is less relevant for a new situation.
Traditional institutions – educational, religious, economic, political – also have an aura of authority.	Traditional institutions of authority are questioned.
The sanctions, or reasons for 'good behaviour' – religious, national – are widely accepted.	The sanctions for conformity are questioned and sometimes rejected as myths.
The young are weak economically and politically.	The young grow stronger economically and politically.

Another summary could be achieved by following young people through their weekly experience and gaining a measurement of the results of social change by asking where their experience is markedly different from that of their parents at the same age. Here we might notice.[25]

a At work – 'new production methods and changing techniques in industry set long experience at a discount and latest training at a premium.' Full employment and inflation have affected the economy and unskilled and semi-skilled workers have reaped the biggest benefits. 'With the rationalization of industrial processes specialization of the work-task has increased, and with it the impersonality of work relation, and a lack of comprehension of work activity.' 'Most young people today are not expected to internalize the "work ethic" of the last century and the religious values with which it was associated.'

b As consumers – They have far more choices, far more to spend and they are subject to increasing advertising pressure; they are fashion-conscious and spending-prone.

c In education – They have more opportunities if they wish to take them. Though they may not have to struggle for economic survival as their parents, yet they may be pressurized into further education because this is one of the surest ways of 'getting on' and 'being somebody'.

d In entertainment – They have their own tastes in music, dancing and films. Vast sums are expended on satisfying those tastes.

e At home – With the growth of places of entertainment, adolescent wealth and teenage culture, probably more of their living takes place outside the home.

Finally, we could attempt our brief summary in yet another way – in fact, by taking three of the main aspects of the 'adolescent task' in our culture and asking how they are generally affected by rapid social change.

a Discovering identity. 'Who am I?' is frequently the unspoken question of adolescence. According to Mays the answer has three parts.[26]

   (1) Who am I for myself? What is to be my self-image?

   (2) Who am I for others and the society? How do others see me and what is to be my place in the adult world? What job should I do?

   (3) Who am I in relation to the world? What is my place in the whole 'creation'? What is the meaning, if any, of my single human life?

On the whole it may be said that the problem of self-identification is harder in a society which is itself uncertain about the identity of the individual.

b Achieving significance. Everybody in a sense 'wants to be somebody' and this need can be felt acutely in adolescence. Youngsters want to establish themselves with their contemporaries and in the adult world. Societies of rapid social change tend to focus status on achievement – that is what is meant by saying that they are meritocratic. This works out well for the unusually talented, who can become pop-stars or soccer idols, or the unusually brainy, who can become university professors. But it bears hardly on those who are (in the felicitous phrase of the Newsom Report) of 'average or less than average ability'. They too easily feel a sense of social rejection and in consequence find the 'adolescent task' harder. Part of the psychological explanation of the various 'deviant' youth groups – skinheads, hell's angels, greasers – is that they are seeking in this way, among smaller contemporary groups, what they do not feel as members of society – identity and significance. A large part of the membership of these groups is composed of 'educational drop-outs'.[27] Excessive devotion to a football team and over-identification with a soccer star no doubt frequently has the same roots. (For a fuller discussion of this point see pp. 100–101).

c Gaining psychological independence. Modern societies differ from earlier predecessors in that they do not arrange opportunities for young people to demonstrate and gain their manhood. In one of Jeffrey Farnol's novels a young man is only allowed to leave home and go off on his travels when he has overcome his father in an arranged fight. The struggle for adulthood is often more complex and confusing for our youngsters. Here lie many family quarrels: the brash challenge of the adolescent, the failure of the adults to understand what is happening, the conflict with those whose support he needs but who may not think they are denying freedom because there are no visible chains.

Rapid social change and the 'youth problem'

All over the contemporary world people seem to be talking about the 'youth problem'. The commonest illustrations are drug-taking, political protest which sometimes uses violence, 'hippie' styles of living, sexual permissiveness, delinquency and the breakdown of relationships with parents.

At the height of the protest season, one can see groups of excited people, old and young, on the Kurfürstendamm in West Berlin, arguing a political point across the generations. Next day perhaps the police will be out with the water cannons. Press lord Springer's property is not safe for long. In Israel, though there is a low incidence of juvenile delinquency and a high level of youthful involvement with the community, educational officials will say how worried they are about the rising generation. Hong Kong parents worry because their children are too much affected by American culture and neglect the Chinese traditions. In Britain politicians have found hostile crowds at university meetings and even suffered the threat of physical violence; on the campus administrative buildings have been temporarily taken over by undergraduates. Nor are misgivings about youth confined to capitalist countries: one can often hear the same kind of talk from older people behind the Iron Curtain, though there is a tight social control of everybody.

There must be a phrase in many contemporary languages for 'youth problem'.

For those who want to understand what is happening to young people today, it is not permitted to take these events at their face value, least of all to accept the valuation which is frequently put upon them by the mass-media of communication. Popular opinion of the young needs careful scrutiny.

We have to ask first how much of this is simply the perennial struggle of the young and the old. Not all of these events can be traced to an extra rebelliousness. Some of it is due to the fact that in many places the young have more power today and in most places their unusual behaviour receives more publicity.

Then we ask what proportion of the youth population are engaged in these various 'deviant' activities. Different answers emerge in different areas. According to reports millions of American youngsters are on 'soft' drugs, but in most British universities only a minority of undergraduates are politically active or even interested. Of course, in the age of the mass-media, deviant behaviour receives far more publicity. Though it is true that a minority of deviants can constitute a threat to a community, yet in Britain and most other countries the vast majority of youngsters are content to be socialized: they are educated, go to work, marry, settle down and raise a family.

Our main concern now is to avoid the clumsy thinking that often goes on about the 'youth problem' whereby things which look alike are lumped together though they are in fact very different, and equally, where whole groups of young people are indicted for the behaviour of a publicized minority.

In particular, if required, we want to refute the unsophisticated notion that any 'unsatisfactory' behaviour of any youngster can be fully described in terms of individual, or even family, morality. As though every juvenile delinquent simply had an extra dose of original sin! Individual behaviour is compounded of social conditioning as well as individual choice and this factor, present in all cases, is unusually prominent in the experience of the young.

Later in this work we enter into more detail both about adult attitudes and the attitudes of young people. Sufficient now to identify the failure to think carefully and fairly about a situation which concerns many of us. At one extreme is the girl student who said to the author that it was good to see young people protesting about anything since this demonstrated that they were not complacent. To which at the time, the proper reply seemed to be that this was a pleasant piece of nonsense – everything surely depended on the validity of the cause for which they protested. At the other extreme are those older people who carry in their minds fixed images of all young people being in a state of perpetual revolt against their elders and their country.

What we are talking about is, in sociological language, 'alienation'. The literal meaning of 'separated from' carries the intention. The 'alienation of the young' means the behaviour of young people which is not according to the common pattern, which may remain, although, as we have seen, it is not so firm or definite in times of rapid social change. 'Alienated youngsters' behave in ways that may be a surprise, an embarrassment or even an affront to the rest of the community.

To clarify our thinking on the subject, there is profit in pondering two thoughts obvious enough but often neglected in the places where men gather to talk over the events of our time.

Not all forms of the alienation of youth are necessarily bad (just as all forms are not necessarily good). There are confrontations when young people are able to look with fresh eyes at society, and they can condemn the compromises and hypocrisies which older people have learned to accept and even grown complacent about. In 1968 a group of students in Birmingham undertook a survey which found that the lives of many old people were threatened by hypothermia; without this investigation presumably the facts would not have been generally known. Youth at its best can ask the devastating question 'Why?': through its youth a nation may have its energies renewed and be saved from complacency, lethargy and snobbery.

4

The second appeal is not to lump together all the expressions of the 'alienation' of youth as though they were exactly alike, reaching back to the same social factors and individual motivations. There are in fact several ways in which they might be grouped. We shall content ourselves now with suggesting brief, tentative divisions in consideration of a larger discussion later in the book about the several groups of young people.

First, there is the vexed question as to how much of the alienated behaviour of the young is 'anti-culture' and how much is 'sub-culture'. The first indicates a deliberate rejection of, 'going against' what adults do, deliberately embracing the opposite. One comment in this area has been that teenagers reject adult hair styles because this is an important matter for adults but their voting behaviour will not differ from that of adults for whom voting is not important! 'Sub-culture' refers to the development of their own style of living – dress, music, entertainment, relationships – because they like it that way and are pressurized into conformity by their contemporaries. The distinction is not merely academic. To many adults it may be useful to say – 'Because that youth has hair reaching down to his shoulders, likes pop music and wears dirty jeans, do not conclude that he is not working hard at his education or place of work, and is not faithful to one steady girl friend, and will not go on to be a useful member of the community – a good husband and father, an industrious worker and a loyal, respectable citizen.' If you so conclude, you may well be wrong!

Second, where the alienation springs from a positive dislike of life in the society where the young have been born, further distinctions may be drawn. One is between the 'socially-rejecting' and the 'socially-rejected'. The first is used to indicate those who judge their society to be at fault in some way and want to change it. These are usually found among the intellectual *élite*, the students. The 'provos' in Holland were, a few years ago, a good example. These were the young, educated Dutch who sought by ingenious means to remedy the ills, as they saw them, in their society. Once they painted white the gates of all the factories in the city which had made arrangements to contribute to the smokeless zone. By contrast, the 'socially-rejected' are far less articulate, sophisticated and politically organized: they feel that life has let them down. Educational processes themselves may have contributed a message that they are second-class citizens. Where prestige is measured by cleverness, reflected in diplomas, qualifications and degrees, they are of low ranking. Youngsters in this group may decide – though not all do of course – to get 'their own back' by acts of delinquency, vandalism, hooliganism and anti-social behaviour. In modern industrial societies, a significant number of juvenile delinquents are educational drop-outs and those who clearly will not gain the rewards of a meritocracy.

Another form of division might be borrowed from R. K. Merton.[28] In describing 'anomie' on the American scene, he states that there are socially-acceptable goals or ends for everybody – to be a success and make money – but there are not for everybody socially-acceptable means of achieving these ends. It is far more difficult, for example, in fact nearly impossible, if you are born a poor Negro. Merton lists five ways in which individuals may respond to anomie thus defined – two of them only concern us here. Individuals may take the retreatist attitude, contracting out of society – the drug addicts, the hippies, the complete individualists, hoboes, nihilists and anarchists may be in this group. Or they may wish to accept some things in their society and change others mostly by constitutional and persuasive methods – these are the constructive revolutionaries. This list is no longer satisfactory since it does no full justice to those revolutionaries who want to destroy present society completely in order to build another, in this view, more humane, less materialistic and less prone to crush the human spirit. But in Merton's division we can recognize young revolutionaries whom we know.

Of course, none of these divisions are absolute or should be applied rigidly – they are merely devices for helping us to organize in our minds many facts which at first look unrelated. In real life situations, the matter is more complex than in any categories we care to invent. The line between 'retreatist' and 'activist' alienation is hard to draw often in a single life. Petty crimes may be politically motivated. Protest marches may satisfy personal emotional needs. A rubber frontier runs between the 'socially-rejecting' and the 'socially-rejected'. Witness the uneasy alliance between political radicals and hippies in California. For co-operation the first have had to abandon part of their seriousness and puritanism, and half-heartedly embrace hedonism; the latter have been compelled to make a show of treating politics seriously.

Nor do these categories introduced above claim to be exhaustive:

rather, they are set forth as a spur to reflection. The 'problem of young people' or 'the alienation of youth' is a subject deserving of more careful thought than it usually commands.

Until it was closed down by the city authorities a few years ago, there was an unusual youth centre in West Berlin. It was founded on the political dissent of the adolescents who crowded its four rooms three nights a week. Drinking lager beer (the profits of which were the main source of income) one could watch, across a smoke-laden room, young wandering political minstrels from all over the world and hear them sing their protest songs. Occasionally, one or two leading politicians braved the audience and had a hostile reception. Fierce political arguments went on all around. To the superficial glance that is what it was – a gathering of young people held together by political dissent. But longer and deeper knowledge disclosed that there were at least three distinct and often opposing groups. There were the nihilists and anarchists for whom 'Mao was too respectable'. There were the Left-wing constitutionalists who wanted to change their society by genuinely democratic means. There were also the older scholars from the grammar schools who were protesting against the authoritarian methods of their teachers. What looked at first glance like a solid block of dissent, proved on closer investigation to contain identifiable parts.

Those who would understand the young will often find similarly that a view which to the unaided eye is a blur of indistinguishable parts begins to have sharper definitions with the aid of intellectual telescope and microscope.

Summary of this chapter

Social change takes place in most societies and affects the lives of most individuals.

Rapid social change affects the lives of individuals more drastically: much changes quickly including values.

Young people who have stopped being children but are not yet fully accepted as adults are among those in the community most affected.

In many ways the mobile society tends to give them more power and freedom, but less support and guidance.

Under modern conditions, rapid social change is linked with other realities which affect the lives of young people – technological changes, meritocracy, mass-media, urbanization.

Socializing agencies like school, home and church are slow to change; they often do not respond quickly enough to support youngsters in the new situation.

Hence at times of rapid social change there is among the young more 'alienation', which takes many forms, including youth culture, crime, drugs and political protest.

Notes

1 The Roundhay Park line, Leeds, for example, inaugurated overhead electric traction in 1891. The last London tram was withdrawn in 1952.

2 Official educational documents in Britain during the nineteenth century could speak quite openly of educating children for their station in life. In the twentieth century this was governed by age, ability and aptitude.

3 The writer recently did this in Sheffield where he was born and later lived part of his adult life from 1942–6. He walked from the Town Hall, through the East End – where he formerly worked – along Attercliffe Common and beyond Tinsley terminus, a distance of five miles. The immediately noticeable changes in twenty years were the disappearance of the famous Sheffield trams and their replacement by buses; the closing of cinemas and churches but the persistence of public-houses; the relative depopulation of the area; and the fact that at Tinsley a whole community seemed to have been sacrificed on the altar of a motorway (the M1). It was an interesting experience because he was able to think even further back – another twenty years – to the time when as a boy he was growing up in Sheffield, and thus he measured social change in two periods. At the earlier time, people referred to Pond Street in hushed tones: it was a labyrinth of small mean houses and the whole area had a reputation for crime and violence. One of the ominous phrases he remembers from his boyhood days is 'The police never go alone into Pond Street but only in pairs.' All the houses have now been pulled down and the area incorporated into the central city development. From Norfolk Street one can see green grass!

4 Though, in fact, relatively little has been published on the subject.

5 'Just as there is a variety of social structures, there is a variety

of principles of historical change.' C. Wright Mills, *The Sociological Imagination*, Oxford University Press, 1959, p. 150.

6 At least in modern societies. And one implication of the dominance of technology in this matter – its effect on the pace of social
change – we examine in a few paragraphs.

7 'Because of the interdependence of the elements of society, change
at any one point is likely to precipitate changes elsewhere.'
Ely Chinoy, *Society: An Introduction to Sociology*, Random
House, 1967, p. 74.

8 Though again not necessarily the only agent even of rapid social
change: one notable exception is invasion. In all probability the
Israelites brought few technological innovations into Canaan but
it looks as though Canaan was never the same again.

9 Kenneth Keniston, 'Social change and youth in America', *Youth:
Change and Challenge*, ed. Erik H. Erikson, Basic Books, 1963,
p. 168.

10 As in the incomparable Stanley Holloway poem-narrative where
young Albert Ramsbottom is swallowed by the lion. When the
matter of compensation is raised, Mrs Ramsbottom asks, 'How
much do you usually pay?'

11 There is a story that a party of Yemenite Jews – a fundamentalist
group – could not be persuaded to enter the aeroplane which
would take them to Israel because 'there is nothing about aero-
planes in the Scriptures'. One of the Israeli immigration officials
pointed to a text in the Prophets which promised that the children
of Israel would return to Jerusalem 'on the wings of eagles'. With
this assurance the migrants happily boarded the planes.

12 A generally accepted view would be that status is a description
of a social position and role is the behaviour appropriate to that
position. Thus 'father' is status and role here is the behaviour
which we think is appropriate for fathers. 'Status' tends to stress
rights – hence its overtones of prestige – and 'role' stresses duties.

13 Though that exists and is confusing. Male and female teenagers
cannot always quickly be distinguished. Parsons are dropping the
habit of wearing the 'dog-collar' except for ritualistic occasions.
Charladies are expensively dressed on their evenings out.

14 Those who hold to a conflict view of human society would not
deny that there is reciprocity in human relationships, a con-
census of some kind. Readers who are interested in this
controversy should read a lucid account of it in Peter Worsley,
Introducing Sociology, Penguin Books, pp. 373–92.

15 Bernard D. Davies and Alan Gibson, *The Social Education of the
Adolescent*, University of London Press, 1967, p. 64.

16 Ely Chinoy, op. cit., p. 364.
17 J. B. Mays, *The Young Pretenders*. Michael Joseph, 1965, p. 19.
18 Cf. *The Autobiography of Bertrand Russell, 1872–1914*, George Allen & Unwin, 1967–8.
19 Kenneth Keniston, op. cit., p. 169.
20 Keniston, ibid., p. 169. And to follow the argument to its logical conclusion it will be '*élite*' youth, i.e. those who go on to full-time higher education, who will be most affected in this age-group: hence the 'students' revolt'.
21 E. M. and M. Eppel, *Adolescents and Morality*, Routledge & Kegan Paul, 1966.
22 This is the main argument magnificently sustained throughout S. N. Eisenstadt's, *From Generation to Generation*, Collier-Macmillan, 1964.
23 *The Youth Service in England and Wales*, (Albemarle Report), HMSO, February 1960, paragraph 68.
24 David Matza, 'Subterranean Traditions of Youth', in *Annals of the American Academy of Political and Social Science*, November 1961, pp. 102–18.
25 The following section owes much to and often quotes Bryan Wilson, *The Youth Culture and the Universities*, Faber, 1970, Chapter 1.
26 J. B. Mays, op. cit.
27 Albert Cohen identified status-seeking as a cause of juvenile delinquency in the USA. Lower-class boys finding themselves at a disadvantage in education and business sometimes took the 'delinquent solution', finding identity and significance in criminal activities. Cf. *Delinquent Boys; The Culture of the Gang*, Collier-Macmillan, 1955.
28 R. K. Merton, *Social Theory and Social Structure*, Collier-Macmillan, 1957.

Suggestions for further reading

Social change and rapid social change

Davis, Kingsley, *Human Society*, MacMillan, 1948, chapter 22.
Johnson, Harry M., *Sociology: a Systematic Introduction*, Routledge & Kegan Paul, 1961, chapter 22.
Linton, Ralph, *The Study of Man*, Appleton-Century, New York, 1936, chapters 18, 19.
(These first three recommendations are about sociological thinking on

the subject of social change: what follows is concerned with
descriptions of societies where we can see the effects of change.)

Briggs, Asa, *Victorian Cities*, Penguin Books.
Cecil, David, *Lord M or the Later Life of Lord Melbourne*,
Constable, 1965.
Central Advisory Council for Education, *Half Our Future*
(Newsom Report), HMSO, 1963.
Frankenberg, Ronald, *Communities in Britain*, Penguin Books.
Trevelyan, G. M., *Social History of England*, Penguin Books.

Effect of rapid social change upon adolescents

Eisenstadt, S. N., *From Generation to Generation*, Collier-Macmillan,
1964, chapters 1, 4, 5.
Eppel, E. M. and M., *Adolescents and Morality*, Routledge & Kegan
Paul, 1966, part 1.
Erikson, Erik H. (ed.), *Youth: Change and Challenge*, Basic Books,
1963.
Bettelheim, Bruno, 'The problem of generations', (chapter 4);
Goldberg, Arthur J., 'Technology sets new tasks' (chapter 6);
Keniston, Kenneth, 'Social change and youth in America' (chapter 9).
Erikson, Erik H., *Identity: Youth and Crisis*, Faber, 1968.
Milson, Fred, *Youth Work in the 1970s*, Routledge & Kegan Paul,
1970, chapters 1–3.
Musgrove, F., *Youth and the Social Order*, Routledge & Kegan Paul,
1964, chapter 7.
Odlum, Doris, *Journey through Adolescence*, Penguin Books, chapter 10.
Wall, W. D., *The Adolescent Child*, Methuen, 1948, chapter 1.
Youth Service Development Council, *Youth and Community Work in
the 70s* (Fairbairn-Milson Report), HMSO, 1970, chapter 3.

3 Youth in many lands

We have seen in the last chapter that rapid change considerably affects the lives of people and that adolescents are among those who are most affected. Care should be exercised however not to allow this admittedly large factor to loom too large in attempts to understand young people in the twentieth century. Even in societies which are alike because they are undergoing rapid social change there are differing features which strongly affect the adolescent experience.

Our present concern is with those variables. In treading this path we are merely following, in a small way, a great tradition which belongs to the history of 'sociological thinking', that is the record of the attempts of men to understand human societies. It has happened many times that thinkers have advanced some theory which appeared to make sense in a most illuminating way of what previously appeared to be a collection of unrelated facts. These thinkers have sometimes, so to speak, fallen in love with their own theories, which have also received wide acclaim and acceptance among others. These theories for a time have hardened into unquestioned dogmas on the subject. But subsequent investigation has shown – not that they were entirely untrue – but that they were incomplete, in the sense that they required modification and qualification. 'A is not always present when B alone is present: C has to be there too.' One brief illustration will suffice. For long it was assumed that the Industrial Revolution in Britain had stripped the family of its functions and that the relatively isolated modern family was the characteristic unit of industrial society. In their stark form both of these propositions are now questioned.[1]

If we spend even a short time in a modern country we may generally notice marked features of the way young people are thought of, treated, expected to behave and educated; and equally marked features of the way in which young people themselves respond to these expectations; and all of this we may find ourselves mentally contrasting with what we know happens to young people in other countries and in particular our own.

This is the procedure we are adopting here: what follows is based largely on the author's observations during visits to several countries to study youth culture there. He hopes he is not putting more weight on personal experience than it will bear, but is supported in his views by what has been written about youth in these societies by observers with longer experience.

Psychological interpretation often begins, and to a large extent continues, with the careful observation of behaviour; in other words, we try to understand what is happening 'inside' people by what they do. Usually the interpretation is instantaneous. If our neighbour at a party goes red in the face we can tell instantly whether this represents an inner state of embarrassment and shyness on the one hand, or anger on the other. All in all there are many signs to help us.

So by looking at what happens to young people in different societies, and seeing how they react, we ask whether this gives us any clues to the experience of being an adolescent in that society. But more than this, our approach takes a sociological turn, and by this is meant, the question is asked, 'Are there any patterns?' Do we have to say that all countries are different in this respect? Or can we also trace similarities? Can we describe a few categories that will help us to organize the material in our minds, to grasp what is happening – even though admittedly they will be rough-and-ready categories? This it seems is possible.

There is one outstanding contrast in this respect. It is the amount of effort which is put into the total education of the young to make them into enthusiastic supporters of the régime. In some countries the youngster is indoctrinated at every point of contact with his society; there is political education in the school; support for the State is sold to him through State-run youth movements which he meets in the school, college, university and factory; all the newspapers, magazines, pictures, radio and television programmes have the same purpose. By contrast, there are modern countries where nobody seems to be bothering very much to secure the involvement of the youngster with the community: it is left to chance, though it is hoped it will happen. In the 'Western' democracies there is little political education of the young.

One of the few exceptions to this is Western Germany, and in Hamburg a few years ago the author came across an incident which illustrates the difference between the two situations. As part of a programme of political education in a youth centre, a series of ex-Nazi films were shown to young teenagers.

The message was intended to be 'those were the bad old days which now we have rejected'. The youngsters saw pictures of Nuremburg rallies; they watched and heard Hitler speak at his most hypnotic and hysterical; they saw Goebbels at his work of propaganda. Their reaction was to hoot with laughter. After they had exhausted themselves with merriment, they turned on the older people and asked, 'How could you have been so stupid to be taken in by this?' They were growing up in another world without the intense indoctrinating pressures of the Nazi régime and the old world was incredible.

This is not to deny for a moment that there are immense socialization forces at work even in those societies which strongly reject totalitarianism and regimentation. (Marxists of course would argue that these are far more subtle forms of social control, they do more to crush the human spirit and they are aspects of *bourgeois* morality and capitalism.) Every society socializes its young. The baby who can of its nature take no thought for others must be turned into the respectable citizen who will realize that you cannot always have what you want when you want it; that your happiness is bound up with pleasing others; that we must all to a degree act as other people hope and expect we will. Society has many agents of the socialization process. Among the first are parents with bowel-training. At an early age, the school reinforces the parents' efforts. Children go to school not merely to acquire knowledge but to learn how to behave in ways that will make them acceptable in their society.

Shipman, writing of the socialization process in schools, points out that it is here we learn our place in life, though this need not mean that our place will not change. And in the school socialization there are at least four elements:[2]

1 Clear definition of appropriate behaviour.
2 Rewards for culturally appropriate behaviour.
3 Punishments to eliminate behaviour which is inappropriate.
4 Maximum exposure to the new culture (of the school).

Neither does the process of socialization finish with childhood. Indeed, in secondary education, it may be said often to take a new turn and receive a fresh emphasis when the image may be that they should put away the childish things of the primary school and be 'broken in'.

Through later years of adolescence, in all societies, the pressures to conform continue, though often in societies with a liberal and democratic tradition, covert and unacknowledged. Adolescents are prepared for work, sex and family roles.

'Parents, teachers, youth leaders and story writers combine forces at the onset of adolescence to demonstrate to boy and girl what it means to become a man or woman, and what rewards one is given for successful performance of roles.'[3]

But between this and the socialization which goes on in what are usually called totalitarian countries there is a difference of degree that amounts to a difference in kind. In the latter it is more sustained, positive, organized and acknowledged. It aims to produce, not passive recipients of the traditional standards of the country, not merely respectable citizens of the country, but active and enthusiastic supporters of the régime. It insists that all the educational influences in the life of the youngsters – home, school, youth organization, mass-media of communication, work situation – speak with the same voice. It focuses attention on the corporate goals, like the good of the State, rather than on individual development.

Eisenstadt has pointed out that in modern countries there are three types of youth groups, that is associations of young people on the basis of adolescent age-groupings. These are (1) the school; (2) the adult-sponsored youth group, like the Scout troop or the Government-run youth centre; (3) the spontaneous youth group which grows up without any adult intervention, when young people simply decide to do things regularly together. Not without significance is the impression that the third type is more commonly found in the 'democracies' than in totalitarian countries. There the social controls are stronger, social education receives more attention and the community involvement of the rising generation is not left to chance.

'The Delegate' and 'Komsomol Island' are two official education film strips that I brought back with me from a visit to Russia. The first – designed for the 'Young Pioneers' of ten to fifteen years of age – is an appealing story of a young boy Alyosha, who at a regional rally made a slip and claimed his group had caught 30,000 rodents, whereas in fact they had caught only 3,000 'destroyers of the harvest'. The speech is reported in the newspapers and back home in Apraksino, Aloysha is in disgrace for boasting and lying. But the whole detachment set to and with the help of older people – including grandfather and the manager of the collective farm – they succeeded in catching 30,000 rodents, thus saving the honour of the Young Pioneers and helping with the harvest. The whole piece is heavily moral; youngsters are taught even at this tender age that they have a serious responsibility, and there are one or two particular emphases like the value of corporate effort and the importance of relying upon the advice and help of older people.

'Komsomol Island' is aimed at the older age group of 15–28. It tells of a group of young men who have volunteered to spend the winter on an Arctic island to conduct a project of scientific research. The plane bringing supplies crashes on the ice and the six Komsomol members display considerable ingenuity in coping with the situation, even storing away the parts of the damaged plane. Again, community service is the dominant theme, with emphasis also upon technical knowledge and skill, the comradeship of young workers, together with a sense of the value of the property of the Workers' State. The concluding strip shows the six Komsomol members standing together in the snow: it carries the sub-title, 'Well, weren't they remarkable lads to winter on Komsomol Island?'

As these are not singular but typical examples of much of the material used in this way, it is perhaps not unfair to comment that – shown to British audiences – they appear strange, as from another world. One feels that the youngsters are being 'got at' in a way that is not usual here: the propaganda is crude, naïve and unsophisticated.

Yet the indications are that the majority of young Russians swallow this ideological food. I travelled on a coach to Kiev with a young student who fortunately for me could speak English. 'Nice city you have,' I remarked by way of passing the time. In reply he launched into an enthusiastic ten-minute lecture overwhelming me with statistics about the number of new houses that had been completed last year and the numbers of books which had been borrowed from the public library. I could not help wondering how long I should have to travel on a corporation bus in Britain to gain a like response of enthusiasm and knowledge from one of our youngsters.

At Moscow University I was involved in a rather contentious seminar in which the young leader of the Komsomol assured me that the students have no wish to criticize Marx, Lenin, the State or their parents. After the seminar I received two messages, though. One from a youngster who assured me that it was not a bit like that really – students in Moscow were the same as the world over. The other was from an obvious party official. The exchange between the Komsomol leader and myself had been fairly heated though there was a delayed action effect on the wrath, due to the fact of each of us having to wait for the translator. The party official apologized because 'the young man had been angry'. 'Not at all,' I replied, 'I like to hear people talk enthusiastically of their views. But I don't agree with much of what he said.' 'Oh!' came the solemn reply. 'He was right in his views but wrong to be angry.'

There is nothing furtive about this 'indoctrination' of the young; it is open and avowed; it follows logically from the ideas and opinions put forward in official Russian documents on the subject.[4]

Youngsters breathe the same ideological atmosphere in other modern Communist States. A youth leader in East Berlin told me that the aim is to have all the educational voices speaking with the same voice to the youngsters. 'That is where my world ends,' sadly remarked an East Berlin girl to me: she was driving me to Checkpoint Charlie for my return to West Berlin and we had come within sight of the Wall. A girl known to me in that city with a brilliant grammar school record was told that she could not gain admission to the medical school at the university unless she joined the Free German Youth Movement which she continued obstinately to refuse to do on account of her private convictions. A Methodist youth group there can operate with the windows uncovered if they are reading their Bibles or saying prayers, but they must pull the blinds down if they have dancing or any other purely social recreation since this would tempt others to join the group. True there has recently been a degree of liberalization, due mainly, one supposes, to the international communication system of youth culture. Even this was granted in a comically rigid way. Older teenagers at youth centres were allowed to play a percentage of pop records of foreign make, from the capitalist *bourgeois* world. And this percentage has gradually increased. Meanwhile the strong emphasis of all forms of education is for enthusiastic commitment to Marxism and the community.

In the mountains of Hungary during the summer months one can see older children working on the railways – this is their reward for having worked hard at school during the previous term.

Our illustrations have been of countries where the authorities are indoctrinating the young with a political or economic creed. No doubt we could have found examples of the 'good life' depicted as the service of a nationalist ideal. Such examples have in fact proved commoner in the twentieth century. Indeed it is by no means always possible to separate nationalistic, political and economic causes to which the young are 'sacrificed'. But the important point is not which cause, or which type of cause is served. We are concerned only to identify those societies whose purpose is to secure the allegiance of the rising generation to a defined creed, rather than being primarily committed to their personal and individual development.

We need spend little time on pointing the contrasts with what happens in many other countries. The strongest pressures upon most youngsters in Hong Kong, for example, seems to come from their parents, who want them to work hard at school so they will gain the rich rewards of a meritocratic society – enter a profession or at least attain a white-collar job. There is no sustained process to persuade most of them to serve a cause. In many a mountain village in Jamaica, the problem of the teenagers is not that various kinds of authority are 'getting at them' to make them into something or to secure their active co-operation; rather it seems that nobody cares enough what happens to them, though perhaps it is only fair to add, that there are those who have the will to care, but lack the means.

Among American middle-class youth, one often has the impression that the clearest message their society is flashing to them is, 'Have a good time. You are only young once. And this is a consumer society.'

In Britain any acknowledged attempt to indoctrinate the young with any kind of creed would be repugnant to those engaged in different forms of education. (This is not to deny that there are frequent latent instances of the exact form of socialization which we have been describing.) It may sound an odd thing to say, inviting instant denial, since there is compulsory religious education in the schools for all those not contracted out by the conscientious scruples of their parents. But what is most significant here is the profound change which is coming, slowly but surely, in the form of religious education, and heralded initially by books on the subject that precede the change in practice.[5] Roughly the change is from the teaching of doctrine to the encouragement of experience which can in the broadest sense be described as religious. Psychological understanding in the teaching is valued more than theological correctness. Religious education is seen to be about 'finding God in your heart' rather than in the heavens; 'life' is more important than scripture or dogma.

Though this may be regarded as a recent development, yet it is entirely consistent with what most people who are professionally engaged in education would say that it was, in other words, its ideal intention. Section 36 of the 1944 Education Act – used in renowned definitions – is typical: 'It shall be the duty of the parent of every child of compulsory school age to cause him to receive efficient full-time education suitable for his age, ability and aptitude.' Nothing there about community involvement. Typical too was the Government pamphlet, *Educational Reconstruction*. This begins by the characteristic stress on child-centred education.

> The Government's purpose in putting forward the reforms
> described in this Paper is to secure for children a happier
> childhood and a better start in life: to ensure a fuller
> measure of education and opportunity for young people and
> to provide means for all of developing the various talents
> with which they are endowed and so enriching the inheritance
> of the country whose citizens they are.

Despite the last phrase, the focus of attention is on the development of the individual rather than the 'good of the State', and the last statement would surprise any educationalist in a totalitarian country by its moderation.

These official documents are old now of course, yet they have been superseded by documents that place the stress in education on individual development rather than on corporate goals. The point in fact is made explicitly in the introduction to the Newsom Report.[6] 'We make no apologies for recommendations which will involve an increase in public expenditure on the education of the average pupils. Their future role politically, socially and economically is vital to our national life, but, even more important, each is an individual whose spirit needs education as much as his body needs nourishment. Without adequate education human life is impoverished.'

Care should be taken to observe that the difference between the two approaches are not absolute. The Russians, for example, would want to claim that they are very interested in what happens to their young people as individuals, and this is substantiated by the evident delight which older people show in the activities of young people. But under questioning they would affirm that the good of the individual is only to be found in loyalty to the whole, that their system is the truth and the rest of the world lies in darkness. Conversely, the British would say that education is not only for personal development but to satisfy the needs of the community for educated and responsible people. Most British reports contain a reference to the youth of the nation being our greatest national asset.

Despite these areas of overlap in the two definitions of educational purpose, the way in which young people are thought of, taught and provided for, differs widely in the two situations.

We move now to examine an aspect of the subject which has already shown its head once or twice in the discussion. When in a community we have the socialization of the young in the sense that efforts are being made to turn them into active supporters of the régime, two factors are commonly present. One is an ideology, that is a system of thought, an interpretation of their life together which receives the official support of the Government and of which no fundamental criticism is tolerated; the other is the availability of sufficient resources to mount the programme for the indoctrination of the young.

An ideology then lies behind the self-conscious process of actively involving the young people in support for the régime such as we find in Russia and other Communist States. What is the meaning for us here of the word 'ideology'? It may be said to be a word that has strayed from its original meaning, 'science of ideas'. In a famous interpretation Karl Mannheim sees it as a description of the way in which the ruling classes rationalize their dominance. 'The concept "ideology" reflects the one discovery which emerged from political conflict, namely, that ruling groups can in their

5

thinking become so intensively interest-bound to a situation that they are simply no longer able to see certain facts which would undermine their sense of domination.'[7]

The word is used here however in a sense closer to common usage. An ideology is a point of view held by people who claim that they have the whole truth not merely for themselves but for everybody else and will use the means at their disposal to impose it upon others. In so far as their power permits them, they pre-empt any open discussion of the fundamental tenets of their creed. On a visit to the national headquarters of the Komsomol, I was assured by a leading official that the Soviet authorities were very much in favour of visits by their youngsters to 'Western democracies' and encouraged these excursions. 'Young people in capitalist countries have much to learn from Soviet Youth.' I asked the obvious question which he found genuinely unexpected and perplexing. 'Do you think Soviet Youth have anything to learn from youngsters in the Western democracies?'

This is not to infer that the Communists are the dark angels of ideological rigidity whilst, say, the Americans are apostles of individual liberty. Anybody who has wandered in the States, particularly south of the Mason-Dixon Line, knows that there is a 'latent ideology' in parts of American society. Some Americans are curiously like Russians in their conversations (blood brothers under the skin) in the sense that they believe that they have a solution of the problems of the human race which has worked well in their country, which will work well for everybody else and is therefore for export. (Only in this case it is a free enterprise economy and not Marxism.) But is there not objectively a difference? The American 'ideology' can at least in certain parts of the Union be subject to intellectual scrutiny, public debate and criticism; it is not ferried along every educational channel; it does not receive monolithic official support. Whatever the impression, faults and hypocrisies of the democracies they have a few in-built self-criticizing devices.

It is precisely the absence of these devices which the visitor to Russia notices during his tours of observation and conversations with officials. And behind this approach lies not merely the neglect of the liberal tradition in education, but, in most cases, its rejection contingent upon the demands of an ideology.

Is the lack of this kind of control of the thinking of young people any more than the fact, as some would affirm, that there are other and subtler ways of controlling the young? Is 'freedom' any more in those societies than a *bourgeois* device, as for example, students of the New Left affirm?[8] We think it is, though this is not to deny that there are covert attempts to control the thinking of young people, a determination not to allow their rebellion to go too far and bureaucratic practices within the educational processes. But it seems that only those who are blinded by ideology will deny that mixed up with dross there is a genuine block of the pure gold of a liberal tradition in the English education theory and practice. It modifies the excesses of the most authoritarian of schoolmasters; it informs more prominently still what is usually written about educational theory and practice. As Neill, a famous figure in English education, has written, 'When I was younger I was more than once called a brilliant teacher . . . even two H.M.I.s said so. I was nothing of the kind. I was doing all the work instead of letting the class do it. I was Billy Grahaming and the poor unskilled boobs were harkening to my gospel when they should have been telling me about it.' Most British teachers, especially the young ones, will respond favourably to such a passage. The Crowther Report,[9] for example, which had much to say about the need for a 'faith to live by', is adamant nevertheless that there are no packaged deals which can be handed around. 'Whatever the reasons neither adults or teenagers are willing nowadays to take very much on authority. . . . The idealism that is latent in all young people can be elicited by those who are scrupulously honest and patiently knowledgeable in their teaching. It is important . . . that no regulations should fetter the directness of their testimony . . .' So say they all, including the Albemarle Report[10] and the Newsom Report.[11] When in 1963, as previously related, Dr Henderson, the Principal Medical Officer to the Ministry of Education, told a meeting of teachers that he would not regard young men and women planning to marry and who have sexual intercourse before they marry as unchaste, he may fairly be regarded as having offended against the accepted norms of his society in this matter and indeed his statement raised a storm of protest in the country. He was however defended in the House of Commons by the Minister of Education, Sir Edward Boyle, in the following words, 'It was the speech of a morally serious man, deeply concerned about modern social problems and deeply concerned about how

we can help young people to form a sense of values for themselves and that seems an approach which should command the
admiration and approval of this House.'

The negative side of this liberal tradition is the absence of an
ideology: less and less are people happy to think that there is one
point of view which can be imposed on the young. If there are
vestiges of an ideology in Britain they are in the broadest sense the
Christian religion. Yet one who completely rejected the Christian
interpretation, Bertrand Russell, wrote these words:[12]

> Where authority is unavoidable what is needed is reverence
> . . . The man who has reverence will not think it his duty to
> 'mould' the child. He feels in all that lives, but especially in
> human beings, and most of all in children, something sacred,
> indeclinable, unlimited, something individual and strongly
> precious, the growing principle of life.

In summary, the effects upon the young of rapid social change
are modified in those countries where there are sustained efforts
to persuade them to support actively the régime. These forms of
socialization rely upon a strong ideology and the weakness of the
liberal tradition of education. This has been illustrated by looking
at Britain where there is no one clear ideology to be accepted and
communicated and where the liberal tradition in education is
relatively strong; it could have been illustrated from other modern
countries. But one does not want to over-paint the contrast.

Most educational systems are both humane and functional, that
is, they aim to serve both the society and the individual: they are
about earning a living – and thus contributing to the wealth of the
country – as well as learning to live – and thus enjoying more
experiences. Part of the difference is how much lip-service is paid
to one ideal or the other. Nevertheless, when all has been said, we
maintain that for most youngsters the difference between being
in one or other type of society is not marginal and usually adds up
to contrasted experiences of adolescence.

The visitor to Russia and most other Communist countries cannot
fail to be impressed by another feature of the life of youth, that is
the scale of the provision which is made for their welfare and
education, at least in urban areas. An educationalist from the West

might be forgiven for envying his colleague in the Soviet Union
for the vast resources which are at his command. This sometimes
becomes apparent from the buildings – the Palace of Youth, the
Palace of Sport, the Palace of Culture. In Moscow, for example,
there is one Palace of Youth which is large enough to require – so
I was assured – the services of 700 full-time youth leaders, which
is almost exactly the same number employed in the whole of
England and Wales in 1958. (And all of it built, I was told, by the
voluntary work of Komsomol members.) In addition, there is
plenty of equipment for a variety of activities and programmes
which offer many opportunities for holidays and camping.

The kind of socialization process which we saw in Russia, then,
depends not merely on an ideology, but on the availability of
resources to support projects to indoctrinate the young. There are
countries in the world where they would not be averse to moulding
the thinking of their youth (despite, as in the case of British ex-
colonies, some effect of the British liberal tradition in education).
In fact, there are many people in these countries who may feel
that this is required since the country has recently acquired self-
government and a strong sense of a national identity needs to be
communicated, but they are held back simply because they lack
the resources. A slight variation on this theme is those places in
the world where in fact the country does have the resources, but
for certain reasons is not willing to use them on the education of
the young.

In many ways Jamaica is an illustration of this form of youth
culture. The country became separate and self-governing in 1962.
After centuries of slavery and colonialism it is vital to help people
to be aware of a 'Jamaican identity'. Nor are the efforts towards this
goal to be despised. A new national anthem has been written. A
large mansion in Kingston has been set aside to house examples of
indigenous Jamaican culture. Central to those attempts must be
that the rising generation should think of themselves as 'Jamai-
cans' and not exiled Africans or emancipated Britishers. Sustained
efforts are made through the channels of education and communication to persuade the younger generation to be proud of and
work hard for their country. No doubt to a degree these efforts
meet with success, but they are considerably hampered by the
poverty of the land. A few years ago, at least, there was only one
place for every two children of primary school age and only one

place for every ten children of secondary school age; there is a high rate of drop-out in primary schools; there are tens of thousands of young male adults who are illiterate, unskilled, unemployed, having lacked a social father. Many youngsters exist in the mountain villages in a condition of marginal poverty, and even more so in the slums of western Kingston. The wealth of a country can be measured perhaps more accurately by the educational skills of the people than by the possession of physical resources: official sources put the illiteracy rate for those over fifteen at 40 per cent. One cannot fail to admire the heroic efforts of many adults in the island to provide the means to help the young people to develop their possibilities and become respectable citizens. Equally one cannot fail to observe their difficulties with inadequate resources. The Youth Development Agency have sponsored youth camps primarily to teach agricultural skills to untrained and uneducated youths, but everybody agrees that there are not nearly enough of them. A similar camp for girls is still at the planning stage.

The picture is much the same in many African countries. A seminar on Youth development in Africa sponsored by the Commonwealth Secretariat, and held at Nairobi in November 1969, found poverty rearing its ugly head again and again to challenge the hopes of educationalists and politicians.[13] 'The seminar considered how the limited funds can be utilized and examined, how the costs of training facilities may be minimized to extend the benefits of training to the maximum number of young people.'[14] The phrase might find a place in similar deliberations in many industrialized countries, but the illustrations which follow make us immediately aware that 'limited funds' here carries another meaning. One suggestion is that labour costs shall be reduced by using trainees to put up their own buildings. (The youths in the Jamaican work camps take some part in growing their own food, making their own clothes, building their roads and dormitories, and servicing their vehicles.) On transport 'the need was stressed for further experimentation on, and increased information on, low-cost animal-drawn vehicles in areas where their use is practicable.'

In Guatemala in 1964 less than 1 per cent of an age group reached university, 5 per cent reach secondary school and 48 per cent are in primary school.[15]

In poor countries educational progress must aim to be vocational in an immediate and practical sense. The same report shows that one of the odd results of educational progress is that it 'harms the economy' in the sense that it produces expectations among youngsters who go to school that they will enter the professions or secure a white-collar job, whereas the paramount need is for agricultural work. We can see this same process at work in Jamaica: many of the youngsters who attend the youth camps (which are ostensibly designed to produce more knowledgeable and skilful workers on the land) in the end do not want to go back to the land – they feel that their education has fitted them for something better. Where poverty presses thus heavily upon the training of youth, there is little room for social education, whether the phrase be taken to mean the enhancement of leisure-time or the active support of the régime. Hence we do not find in poor countries, generally speaking, the elaborate and sustained programmes of indoctrination and socialization such as we find say in Russia and East Germany.

Basic wealth or poverty, the size of the Gross National Product, are clearly determining factors in the nature of the adolescent experience. A related question, of course, is how many there are to share the cash, in other words, what proportion of the population is young. In developing countries for example, it is common for more than half the population to be under fifteen.

Elsewhere the problem may be not that there is a lack of resources but that there is an unwillingness to use any major part of them for the welfare and education of the young. The only place in the world personally known to me that fits this description is Hong Kong. At present the colony enjoys a booming economy. The 1969–70 financial year ended with a Government revenue surplus of over thirty million pounds. Yet for the majority of the population life is a struggle. Wages are low, hours are long and social benefits are minimal. Cheap labour is believed to be essential to the maintenance of Hong Kong's economic position and her advantage as a free port. Yet the effect of this on young people is plain to see. Education is highly prized since it leads to the white-collar job or the professions and suits the high prestige given to scholarship in the Chinese tradition. But for the poorer sections of the community, educational opportunities are severely restricted. 'A widowed middle-aged house servant, from a total income of £30 a month, has to pay £14 for the secondary schooling of her three children. This does not include the purchase of text-books and clothing and the children's bus fares. At £30 a month, this 'amah' is making as much as an unskilled male industrial worker who might have as many as ten children.'[15] Hong Kong is the only place where I have visited a youth centre and seen 'doing your homework' as the most popular activity of the evening. Doubtless part of the demand for room at tables to work at their books was due to the restricted conditions of their homes, but not all. Many youngsters face strong pressures put upon them to work hard and get on with their work and make progress in an education which is being dearly bought by their parents at scarcity prices.

What has been suggested so far in this chapter can be expressed in three equations: where S = the socialization process to the degree that youngsters are admittedly and officially indoctrinated to accept political commitment; where R = the availability of substantial resources for adequate programmes for the young; where I = the ideology, or the 'myth' which lies behind the in-doctrination process; thus:

$$S+ = R+ \text{ and } I+$$
$$S- = R- \text{ and } I+$$
$$S- = R+ \text{ and } I-$$

This it must be repeated is only a rough-and-ready division de-signed to help us to make a preliminary division of the vast amount of unrelated material which comes to us from different countries. And the formula is not to be pushed too far nor should we ask those equations to bear an impossible weight. What in fact we dis-cover is that though our categories will help us to go part of the way to understanding, yet in many countries there are individual features which profoundly affect the experience of young people there. It could be climate or the persistence of a strong religious tradition or the fact of one trade like fishing to which the whole economic life is geared. Or more commonly, it can be an unusual political situation which casts long shadows over the teenage scene. Of this situation there are two good contemporary examples.

West Berlin and Israel are unlike in many ways. But they share a sense of siege: they are both 'democracies under pressure' in that they are committed to a form of government which permits public discussion of all issues, but they are both at the flashpoints of history and their survival depends on recruiting supporters for the régime from a new generation. In their attitudes to the young, they may both be said, in the terms of our equations to show that 'S$+$ $=$ I$-$ and R$+$' if the stakes are high enough. In both places the leaders display comparable attitudes to the young: they want them to be free men who think about and decide issues for themselves but they want them to reach a conclusion which assures the persistence of the present political structures. If they indoctrinate, they always do it with a bad conscience.

West Berlin has been described by Western sympathizers as 'an island in the Red Sea' and as 'a capitalist shop window in the Communist world'. The city fathers are naturally preoccupied with preserving their freedom and not being absorbed into the Communist world. Strategically, of course, their position is weak. There is an avowed programme of political education sponsored by or supported by government funds, and those funds are lavish, drawing not only from the wealth of a large industrial city, but also from Federal sources. But to be frank, 'political education' in West Berlin means, understandably, 'anti-Communist education'. 'What keeps me awake at night', a leading educationalist in the city commented to me, 'is whether we can persuade a new generation to believe in and, if necessary, fight for West Berlin.'

Hence, for this and other reasons, the political situation plays a prominent part in the lives of West Berlin youth. One night in a jazz saloon in the city I asked a group of young visitors, most of them about seventeen or eighteen years of age, what they thought of the political situation in West Berlin. They laughed, shrugged their shoulders and said they were not really interested. 'There is always love.' Later that same evening I related the incident to a group of young West Berlin trade unionists with whom I was having a general discussion. One of them commented that was all right but politics could affect your love life: his girl friend lived in East Berlin. This is not to infer that any majority of young people react in the same way to these pressures. Some are indifferent, other react by strong rejection of the teaching of the authorities and nowhere have I seen the students' revolt so extreme, determined and violent. But politics plays a big part in the lives of West Berlin youngsters. Anybody can join in political conversations with young people in the cafés at night.

In Israel, a State surrounded by hostile Arab forces, some of whom are avowedly dedicated to her destruction, one might think the stakes are even higher and hence the pressures stronger. One aspect of community involvement is, of course, military service for both girls and boys. 'I am very worried about our young people', said an Israeli official. At first I could not understand that. They appear healthy, strong, intelligent and, above all, committed to the nation. But he went on, 'Israel has no future unless we can produce another generation of pioneers, workers and warriors.' A few years ago a decision was taken to subsidize the youth programmes of all political parties on the grounds that 'to have any political philosophy is better than negativism'.

Significantly, West Berlin and Israel are among the few 'democracies' where there are officially supported programmes of political education for the young. In Israel, the recent developments of the 'Black Panther' movement modify but do not reverse this view.

What has gone before in this section does not pretend of course to be a full picture of what is 'happening to young people in modern countries', nor is it a representative picture. Either of these exercises would be a massive undertaking of research and analysis. Even a representative picture is far beyond the knowledge and experience of the present writer. Our purpose is more modest. In fact, it is to provide an international backcloth against which the details of British youth will stand out in sharper definition.

Few people will deny that Britain is passing through a period of rapid social change. This could be tested in many ways – forms of entertainment, dress, transport and social customs – and though change can be seen as a promise and not a threat, yet there are aspects of change which unsettle the individual and add difficulties to his life-task. Among those most affected are young adults.

In Britain, as we have seen, there is no one political philosophy which is pushed upon the young and though religious instruction in schools is 'compulsory', one no longer has to be a Christian or to hold any other religious views to be socially-acceptable in Britain. There is 'no indoctrination' because there is not one official 'ideology'. So in terms of the formula, the equation for Britain is $S- = I-$ and $R+$. For, relatively speaking, there are enough resources for the welfare and education of the young and those resources are made available for the purpose. Of course, dedicated educationalists will argue again and again that too low a percentage of the national income is spent on education; that this is disastrous in human terms since one consequence is that many men and women do not develop all their possibilities and live impoverished lives; that it is disastrous from the national point of view; as a trading nation in a technological and competitive age, we cannot afford not to spend more on education, since to fail to do so is to weaken our resources. There is undoubtedly substance in both these arguments. Nor would we want to deny gross inequalities in the educational system or that educational opportunity often remains obstinately class-structured so that it seems sometimes as though the bright youngster from the middle-class home has all the winning cards in his hands. But, relatively, the resources are there and are made available. A visit to any developing country makes Britain look like the land of educational opportunity.

Moreover, though many would think there is much room for further improvement, there have been significant changes recently. The following table tells part of the story.

Table 1   Percentage of children of different age groups attending primary and secondary schools in England and Wales, 1950 and 1967[17]

Age	1950	1967
5–10	99	99
11–14	99	100
15	30	66
16	14	30
17	7	16
18	2	5

Later figures would show further improvement in the same direction; each year more children stay on at school beyond the required minimum age.

Another sounding of like nature is the increasing amount of public money that was spent on the Youth Service in England and Wales during the last decade. Central government authority expenditure in this area rose from £299,000 in 1959–60 to £1·9 millions in 1967–8. Local authority expenditure rose from £2·56 million to £10 millions in the same period. In addition, 3,000 building projects in Youth Service from 1960 to 1968 cost £28 million.

We have said that the position of young people in a modern society can be understood not only in terms of the rough formula worked out above, but also in the light of general overriding factors in that society. In the case of British youth there appears to be two: the first we judge to be of bigger influence than the second.

The generation of teenagers growing up in Britain today are children of the 'Welfare State' and a land where wealth and opportunity have been more widely distributed. This is not to infer that they are of all men to be envied or that the enlargement does not in some ways create its own problems for them. But it is in this area that there lie the most frequent contrasts with the experiences of their elders and often of their parents. Many a father who has striven to improve his social position by heroic efforts of self-education or who now realizes how grave have been the restrictions placed upon his opportunities by the lack of early education, sees his children given chances that were unheard of in his day. Older people may sometimes be forgiven for thinking that the primrose path is carefully pruned for the progress of the young. (Of course, this is not to deny that there are among all sections of the population pockets of serious deprivation, that in many respects these pockets are large and that a frustrating paradox of the increasingly affluent society is that the very poor become poorer.)[18]

Largely through the provisions of a Welfare State in complementary services the young in Britain today as a whole and by contrast with the two generations which have gone before them display the following features:

1 They are physically in better shape – healthier, fatter, taller.
    Some of the reports of medical officers of health from the thirties – particularly with reference to malnutrition, rickets and anaemia – read today like statements from the Dark Ages.
2 They are maturing physically at an earlier age.
3 They have more energy.

4 They are better educated and have bigger educational prospects.
5 They have bigger expectations of what life can bring them.
6 They have more spending power.[19]

In 1938, according to a Ministry of Labour survey, boys
between 15 and 20 who were at work earned an average of
26/– and girls 24/– a week. Most of this money seems usually
to have been handed to parents, leaving only a few shillings
weekly for discretionary spending. Before the war, then, it is
roughly true to say that adults had a monopoly of spending
power; and adolescents in work were economically dependent.
By comparison, in mid-1958 youths between the same ages
earned an average of £5·12. and girls £5·6. a week . . . the
real earnings of both sexes have increased on an average by
about one half since before the war (which is double the rate
for adults) and their real discretionary spending seems to
be roughly twice what it was before the war.

Clearly these figures are wildly out of date now but the trend has
been in the same direction.

If a 'teenager' is an unmarried person between fifteen and
twenty-five, there were about six million teenagers in Britain in
1965 and their gross income was £2,515,000,000, about 9 per cent
of the present income of the country. According to a survey by
Dr Mark Abrams the following table is an account of their personal
expenditure in 1965:

Table 2   Personal expenditure of teenagers in Britain in 1965

	Boys shillings weekly	Girls shillings weekly	Total annual expenditure £m	As % of all consumer spending
Clothes	12	20	245	15·7
Footwear	3	5	60	17·2
Meals, snacks out	13	4	125	18·4
Cigarettes	9	4	105	10·5
Holidays	6	5	85	8·0

Table 2 (cont.)

	Boys shillings weekly	Girls shillings weekly	Total annual expenditure £m	As % of all consumer spending
Vehicles (including running costs)	7	1	65	4·0
Records, record players, portable radios	4	1	40	35·0
Cosmetics and shampoos	1	3	30	20·0
Hairdressing	1	2	25	23·1
Cameras, sports goods, watches and pens	2	1	25	13·0
Books, magazines	1	1	15	13·6
Other items (including savings)	51	28	650	3·7
	110	75	1,470	6·0

7 They devote more time and energy to the pursuit of pleasure, and this not only because they have bigger spending power than those who have gone before them, but because commercial interest and technological changes join to produce opportunities of enjoyment; combined with this is the strengthening of hedonistic values, that is the view that it is a right, nay a duty, to enjoy oneself.

8 All this leads to the existence of what is called 'a youth culture'. Among sociologists this is much fought-over ground. Is there such a thing as 'youth culture'? Or have we imagined it? And how much of it is 'anti-culture', that is the deliberate rejection of adult values? Thus it has sometimes been pointed out that young people's behaviour does not differ significantly from adults in areas where there is no strong adult feeling or commitment. On this view

important aspects of what we call 'youth culture' are no more than the determination of the new generation to be different from the older generation.

Fortunately, we do not have to enter into this controversy in any depth;[20] we are concerned only to point to a fact which is disclosed by daily observation. There is a style of life in our country commonly associated with young people and which is recognizably different from the life-styles of the rest of the community, and it includes at differing levels of intensity, dress, entertainment and general attitudes. 'With this means at their disposal they [teenagers] are able to enter into a symbiotic relationship with the commercial marketeers to create and enjoy the symbols of a characteristically adolescent culture.'[21]

9 Whilst in this book we are not devoting attention to the real difference in the social position of male and female adolescents – which is a separate and immense subject – we should pause here to notice a widely-held view among those who have thought seriously about the subject. It is that on the whole youth culture is likely to help the girl, more than the boy, to adjust to an adult role in society, and that parts of it are in fact a preparation for the female adult role. This is because youth culture centres on entertainment and as Coleman has argued,[22] 'For adolescent girls pop songs are consistent with and reinforce the "romantic role" which they are expected to play, while songs have not such functions for boys.' Not that 'pop' culture is without possibilities of tension for the girl and may bring her into conflict with parents; and there are indications that girls, both in this country and the USA., are more exposed to it than boys; but there are many aspects which are consistent with the development which others expect of her and which she has come to expect of herself. Teenage culture has probably contributed to the trend towards earlier marriage in Britain. The male is both probably less influenced by 'pop' culture and finds within it more conflict with what is expected of him since society's emphasis is to prepare him for the adult work role.[23]

10 Finally, the young in Britain may be said to have gained in political power. This does not mean that they have acquired larger influence with organized political parties. In fact, they are there mostly inconspicuous by their absence, though in this, as in other matters, they do not stray prominently from adult habits. (Of thirty-six million voters in Great Britain, nine million do not vote

at general elections and a further fifteen million do not vote at local elections. Four million people are actively involved in running the political parties.)

Youthful membership of political parties is roughly:

Young Conservatives aged 15–30	120,000
Young Liberals aged 15–30	12,000
Young Socialists aged 15–25	25,000

The National Opinion Poll survey of 1964 estimated that 5 per cent of the twenty-one to twenty-five age group belonged to a political party. The Campaign for Nuclear Disarmament was the most significant political gesture of the young in the post-war period but it did not conform to political party structure.[24]

The word 'power' might be sufficient to describe what is meant here, but 'political power' is used to indicate that the young have become more important in the total life of the country. This relates to their improved economic strength, and as consumers they are constantly taken into account and wooed by commercial interests. They are more independent, less under the control of older people, including their parents and they adopt some aspects of adult behaviour at an earlier age (the Latey Committee found that their youthful witnesses identified themselves as adults at seventeen). They have now a legal recognition of their adulthood at eighteen, including the right to vote, which means, among other things, that there are voters in the sixth form.

The last ten sections are variations on our theme: that teenagers have improved and strengthened their position in the community and gained more possibilities of influence. However, to complete the picture of 'the outstanding features of youth in Britain', a counter-balancing feature has to be noted.

It has been put in many ways largely depending on the personal point of view of the observer. One way of saying it is – 'People in Britain are uncertain of the place of young people in society partly because they are uncertain of the place of Britain in the World.'

The first part of the statement – which would receive far wider support than the second – we examine first.

Adults are often depicted as being universally 'for' or 'against' youth; more commonly it appears they are confused and indecisive. (We examine adult attitudes to the young in more detail later.) Davies and Gibson see adolescents as among the marginal people in our society. 'A boy or a girl who has left school and yet is neither 21 nor married is an enigma. His place in the total system is not clear, for he is neither totally a child nor totally accepted as an adult.'[25] There is a lot of fine talk about giving youth their head but in practice they are often treated as an inconvenient perplexity. In modern, industrialized, fast-changing societies the young face the same situation that confronts the old – nobody seems to know quite what to make of them and what part to give them. There lies part of the reason for the frequent bond of understanding that we can observe in many places between grandparents and their grandchildren.

For both groups (as we have seen in the case of adolescents) it was far different in earlier, simpler, smaller, agrarian, more static societies. Materially life was much poorer, but neither young nor old were left in doubt as to their rights and duties, their place in the scheme of things.

The conflict and indecisiveness reinforces any inner uncertainty that the youngster may be experiencing. A lot of our behaviour is socially defined, that is in many, perhaps most, areas, we behave as people expect us to behave given the facts of our social position, including age. The 'dilemma' of youth in Britain has been expressed in different ways, and some too emotional and paternalistic for the taste of many thoughtful observers. Thus it has been said, 'We have been able to give the rising generation everything except a faith to live by.' But nobody would accuse Davies and Gibson of being either emotional or paternalistic; they see this uncertainty about the place of youth as a source of suffering for them: 'Young people fundamentally are somewhat puzzled and hurt by their evident estrangement, their statelessness. Much of what we may see as 'teenage culture' is an elaborate disguise of this hurt, which they no more wish to advertise to others, especially adults, than to themselves.'[26]

The rest of the argument will encounter heavier fire. It is the proposition that this role-ambiguity, both for and about young people in Britain, is not only as we have seen, a phenomenon associated with an era of rapid social change, nor can it be wholly explained as the break-up of a 'firm background' against which individuals could formerly measure their lives, but role-ambiguity about youth in Britain is linked with role-ambiguity about Britain. Part of the identity of the individual comes from seeing himself as

6

part of the national whole – the Welsh and Scots are still more able to do this than the English – but on the whole it is much more difficult when the national image is constantly changing and/or is uncertain and/or has in any case been diminished.

The Albemarle Report saw this as an important feature of youthful experience at the close of the 1950s.[27]

> Today adolescents live within a world sharply divided
> into two immense blocks of power: and a world constantly
> under the threat of nuclear catastrophe. In addition, their
> own country's power and international status, once so
> great and indisputable, are now less easily assured. These
> issues may only be made articulate by a few. We are
> persuaded, nevertheless, that they are felt to be immediately
> behind the small stage of many an adolescent's activities,
> like a massive and belittling backcloth.

This is the present judgment though it is disputed by many. The most frequent objection is that the world role and position is not a salient part of the feelings of most adolescents in this country. They are supremely indifferent, being preoccupied with growing up and enjoying themselves. We think this may prove to be a superficial view. It does not follow that people are unaffected by realities which they are not always putting into words, and even appear not to want to put into words. On the positive side can be put the fact that in many places in the world – admittedly often under pressure of political events – the young people have a stronger sense than ours of national identity; that in some places – notably in Soviet Russia – the young people seem to be looking forward to a 'Golden Age' for their people which lies in the future, whereas in Britain it is much commoner to find young people looking into the past for the 'Golden Age' of their country; that one can naturally assume that some of the facts of Britain's diminished and uncertain role in the world will have 'rubbed off' on youngsters. In history lessons at school, they have heard of the 'Empire on which the sun never sets' and many realize that what is left is an embarrassing remnant. They have heard through different news media of the economic problems of their country and the need to borrow money abroad. They are not unaffected by the political arguments which go on among adults concerning the part Britain has to play in the world, arguments say about the

Common Market or whether we should have troops east of Suez.

Our view is then that the role-ambiguity of adolescents is not unrelated to the role-ambiguity of Britain. If the trumpet shall give an uncertain sound, who will follow?

Notes

1 Cf. Peter Worsley, *Introducing Sociology*, Penguin Books, Part II, chapter 3.
2 M. D. Shipman, *Sociology of the School*, Longmans, 1968, p. 61.
3 Cyril Smith, *Adolescence*, Longmans, 1968, p. 36.
4 Cf. Brian and Joan Simon (eds), *Educational Psychology in the U.S.S.R.*, Routledge & Kegan Paul, 1963.
5 Cf. R. J. Goldman, *Readiness for Religion*, Routledge & Kegan Paul, 1965;
   H. A. Loukes, *Teenage Religion*, S.C.M. Press, 1961.
6 *Half our Future* (Newsom Report), Central Advisory Council of Education (England), HMSO, 1963.
7 Karl Mannheim, *Ideology and Utopia*, Routledge & Kegan Paul, 1954.
8 See later in this book for a longer description of the beliefs and attitudes of 'students of the New Left'.
9 *Fifteen to Eighteen* (Crowther Report), Central Advisory Council for Education, HMSO, 1959.
10 *The Youth Service in England and Wales* (Albemarle Report), Ministry of Education, HMSO, 1960.
11 Op. cit.
12 Bertrand Russell, *Principles of Social Reconstruction*, Allen & Unwin, 1916.
13 Cf. *Youth and Development in Africa*, Commonwealth Secretariat, 1970.
14 Ibid., p. 57.
15 UNESCO, 1965, pp. 17–19.
16 *Observer* colour magazine, 6 December 1970.
17 *Statistics of Education*, vol. I, 1967, and vol. I, 1961, quoted by P. Worsley, *Introducing Sociology*, Penguin Books, p. 70.
18 Cf. Alec Clegg and Barbara Megson, *Children in Distress*, Penguin Books.
19 *The Youth Service in England and Wales*, op. cit.
20 References for those who wish to pursue this point further:
   Cyril S. Smith, 'Roles, status and youth culture', *Studi di Sociologia*, 5;

M. Schofield, *The Sexual Behaviour of Young People*, Longmans, 1965;

Bryan Wilson, *The Youth Culture and the Universities*, Faber, 1970.

21 J. B. Mays, *The Young Pretenders*, Michael Joseph, 1965, p. 33.

22 J. Coleman, *The Adolescent Society*, The Free Press, New York, 1961.

23 This paragraph owes much to a paper read by Dr Cyril S. Smith at the West Berlin seminar on youth work in April 1969.

24 Cyril S. Smith, *Adolescence*, Longmans, 1968, pp. 79–80.

25 Bernard D. Davies and Alan Gibson, *The Social Education of the Adolescent*, University of London Press, 1967, p. 72.

26 Ibid., p. 73.

27 Op. cit., p. 29

Suggestions for further reading

About the socialization process as a whole

Davis, Kingsley, *Human Society*, Macmillan, 1948, chapter 8.

Young people in some other modern countries

Africa
Youth and Development in Africa, Commonwealth Secretariat, 1970.

Hong Kong
Jarvie, I. C. (ed.), *Hong Kong*, Routledge & Kegan Paul, 1969.
Milson, Fred, *Youth Programmes in Hong Kong*, Westhill College of Education, Birmingham.
Annual Reports of the Boys' and Girls' Clubs Association of Hong Kong.

Israel
Bentwich, Joseph, *Education in Israel*, Routledge & Kegan Paul, 1965
Leisure Time and Delinquency. A Research Proposal, Ministry of Education, Youth Department, State of Israel, 1961.

Jamaica
Clarke, Edith, *My Mother Who Fathered Me*, Allen & Unwin, 1966.
Milson, Fred, *Youth Programmes in Jamaica*, Westhill College of Education, Birmingham.
Copies of *Torch*, journal of the Ministry of Education, Jamaica.
Annual Reports of the Youth Development Agency, Jamaica.

USA
Erikson, Erik H. (ed.), *Youth: Change and Challenge*, Basic Books, 1963.
Mays, J. B., *The Young Pretenders*, Michael Joseph, 1965, chapter 7.
Smith, Ernest A., *American Youth Culture: Group Life in Teenage Society*, The Free Press, New York, 1962.

USSR
Simon, Brian and Joan (eds), *Educational Psychology in the U.S.S.R.*, Routledge & Kegan Paul, 1963.
Bereday, George Z. F. and Penner, Jann, *The Politics of Soviet Education*, Praeger, New York, 1960.

Youth in Britain

General features
Mays, J. B., *The Young Pretenders*, op. cit.
Milson, Fred, *Youth Work in the 1970s*, Routledge & Kegan Paul, 1970, chapter 3.
Wilson, Bryan, *Youth Culture and the Universities*, Faber, 1970.
Youth Service Development Council, *Youth and Community Work in the 70s* (Fairbairn-Milson Report), HMSO, 1970, chapter 3.

On the proposition that the 'material' position of young people in Britain has improved
Hemming, James, 'Young People Today', a paper read at a Council of Europe Seminar held at Leicester College of Education, 1964.

On the proposition that Britain finds it difficult to offer clear guidance to its adolescents
Davies, Bernard D. and Gibson, A., *The Social Education of the Adolescent*, University of London Press, 1967.

4 Young Englanders

This title, though not entirely satisfactory, is chosen deliberately to describe the young generation in this country. One aspect of our present confusion is that it is not easy to find the right and acceptable term to describe the age-group we have in mind. 'Teenagers' has undertones of disapproval; 'adolescents' sounds clinical; 'youth' comes to define younger groups and is likely to be rejected by those of seventeen and over, though 'young' is still acceptable.

'Young Englanders' is intended to suggest that we are thinking of those who are in many ways like the rest of us and to be seen as members of the community, but distinguished by the fact that they are a separate age-group. 'Englanders' attempts to do justice to a conviction of the writer that what is written in this chapter would in general not be quite so true of young people living in Wales and Scotland. In both those countries, particularly in the rural districts, there seems to be a stronger sense of national identity which modifies the judgment to be expressed.

So far we have been thinking in the most general terms of society, adult attitudes to the young and the attitudes of the young people themselves. A reader could be forgiven for thinking that we have suggested that there is in Britain 'one society', 'one adult attitude to the young' and 'one adolescent'. Clearly this is not so. There are different 'societies' in the one country; for example, there are important differences in the style of life among people who live in different parts of the country, and also, noticeably, in rural and urban areas. These are not without significance for our subject, since these cultural differences will be reflected in the experiences of young people growing up in those areas. (There are parts of the country where parental authority is stronger than elsewhere and where, as a result, the behaviour of young people and the choices they make are much more controlled by home and family.) Again, adults differ widely in the ways in which they think about, relate to and behave with young people. To this judgment clearly they bring the 'whole of themselves', that is, their total personality and what they think about life generally. (It is tempting sometimes to believe that on no other occasion do we reveal ourselves so completely as when answering a question like, 'And what do you think about the young people in Britain today?')

Young people no less – obstinately and fortunately – refuse to be
fixed in neat categories: most of them insist on being their unique
selves. That is why the sweeping generalizations about the young,
in which adults often indulge, are unconvincing and unsophisticated. Usually they are attempts to indict a whole generation:
'young people show no consideration today' is one example. This
is to think in stereotyped images; it is to judge every single
member of a group by conclusions you have reached about the
whole group. Another facet of this attitude is to stereotype the
concept of 'adolescence' as distinct from fitting an individual
youngster into a preconceived pattern. 'Adults have gradually
come to assume that all those to whom the word "adolescent" may
be applied are different and distinct from the rest of adult society
in almost every respect, whereas in fact the word refers precisely
and particularly to one particular respect only in which they are
different . . . To see as largely the same everyone whose age happens to be in the teens is unmistakably to over-simplify. Experi-
enced teachers and youth workers are rarely impressed by such
generalizations since they are repeatedly frustrated by rigid age-
groupings and made aware of discrepancies between develop-
mental age (the only significant age for social education) and the
chronological age of their adolescent clients.'[1]

This chapter then seeks to analyse in more detail the different
'societies' and groups of adults with which adolescents have to
deal, as well as the different groups of adolescents. Even so, experience teaches us that the present treatment may well run into
the criticism that it is too clinical, an attempt to force individuals
into categories and an academic disregard of the refreshing uniqueness of each young person in the land. And the criticism would be
valid and even destructive if what is to be written here pretended
to give a complete account of any single youngster. For an individual life is subject to diverse pressures, many of which may
themselves be highly individual, like the family, the friendship
group, the street and neighbourhood, the influential friend or
relative – and most of these we have no space for adequate regard.[2] We are concerned with the more general collective features.
Moreover, it would certainly be the view of the present writer,
that whatever prominence we give to the social moulding of personality, people in fact are not merely 'vegetables', created by their
environment; they have a small hand at least in the shaping of

their own destiny, the building of their own personality. Since we recognize that every adolescent is uniquely different from every other, what is written here is at least not intended to be clinical or to suggest that human beings can be parcelled up and labelled. Sociologists and social investigators are found not always to appreciate the rightness and the strength of the instinctive dislike that many people have of becoming a statistic. They suspect, and often with justification, that too much will be made of one fact that is learned about them, that they will be lumped together with others who happen to share that characteristic and that consequently their humanity and dignity are diminished.[3]

But what seems equally true is that people are not only different from each other, but in some important respects they may be alike, and to identify their common characteristics is not one whit to deny their uniqueness. More than that – to grasp their common features is part of the process of understanding them better and hence supports the skill of the educator. (It is this insight which lies behind the expansion of the social worker's role from that of a caseworker – concerned almost exclusively with a single client – to include elements of group work and community work.)[4]

Young Englanders – what are they for society as a whole ?

In the language of sociology, a 'norm' is what is expected, what is a socially-acceptable attitude or act. It need not be the same as what people are thinking or doing. In most human societies there is a fair measure of hypocrisy in the sense that people pretend to agree with the norm when privately they think and act differently – a norm relates to a view which we should not hesitate to express in the presence of a stranger.

What are the norms about adolescents in Britain? What is 'public opinion' about how they should behave, about what are 'correct' adult opinions, about how the community as a whole should treat them both in provision and control?

We have noted already that there is a confusion and uncertainty in this realm. At a time of rapid social change some of the established norms of a community are questioned, undermined and changed. One imagines that in earlier, smaller and static societies when adults gathered together to talk there were not usually major disagreements on how the young should be treated. Our present 'normlessness' on this matter can be measured in several places. One is if we think about ourselves as brought into touch with a stranger with whom we have to make conversation – say, at a cocktail party or on a railway journey. We are inclined to cast around in our minds for 'safe' subjects or if a controversial matter is introduced, we are tentative in the expression of views, not being able to predict the views of the other since we know there are strongly-held divergent views on these matters. In those situations we might well conclude that 'youth in Britain' was a subject to be avoided or handled carefully. One can test the uncertainty at another point. From time to time an author will bring together and summarize the reports, official and semi-official, which have been written over a number of years concerned with the education of the young, and here the contradictions appear. (A good example is the first chapter of E. M. & M. Eppel's book *Adolescents and Morality*, published by Routledge & Kegan Paul.) There is no major aspect of human behaviour or interpretation of the mystery of human life about which there are not contrary views in our society. Clearly 'youth' will be affected by this general uncertainty and also because 'youth' is one of the topics on which there are a variety of views. Linked with this is another reason why, in a situation like ours, older people are often perplexed by, 'do not know what to make of', the young.

Our understanding of any other human being or group of people is facilitated when we have had the same or comparable experiences. Then with good reason we may say, 'I know how you feel.' Perhaps it is worth stressing that the experience need not be exactly the same, but can be congruent. Thus in order to be able to talk sympathetically to a boy who has just been thrown over by his girl friend, one need not have been jilted; it is enough to have known the feeling of rejection.

Now it is precisely the conviction and the misgiving that there are not common areas of experience between older and younger people in our society which – perhaps unjustifiably – lie behind the phenomena which are loosely called 'the generation gap' and 'generational tension'. Older people may feel that youngsters are growing up in a different world, a world of transistor radios and space-travel and changing standards, and that they cannot use their own recollections of adolescence to understand today's youngsters, and that 'I know how you feel' carries less conviction.

This is reinforced by the opinion of many young people that their elders in fact cannot understand present circumstances and that, for example, there are few points of contact between their own adolescence and what their parents knew at the same age.

Despite much present confusion, however, we are about to suggest that there are one or two fairly widespread elements – complementary and perhaps, even contradictory – about the way in which public opinion survives on this subject. What follows are four frequent expectations about the relation of our society and young people. The moderate expressions of any one of them would not call for strong dissent or cause the raising of eyebrows in any gathering of reasonable men and women.

1   That the community has a responsibility towards its youth. There is nothing new in this norm: it has been a sentiment of the British for a long time that the young should have the maximum support and encouragement – as long ago as the eighteenth century educational pioneers like Hannah More and Elizabeth Fry relied upon this fact – but the sentiment has been strengthened in the twentieth century by two tendencies. The first is the disposition to blame society for the troubles of the individual rather than to locate the problem in any lack of effort on the part of the individual. It is common today to think of people as 'victims' rather than 'sinners'. The second tendency is a developing egalitarianism which persuades us that the privileges of life should not be the preserve of a minority, but are to be shared by all.

Young people being vulnerable and inexperienced are more likely to be the recipients of those hopeful expectations. Many parents are motivated by the wish to give their children a 'better start in life than we had'. People who may on other occasions be critical of the habits and outlook of the rising generation are quite genuinely shocked when they hear about young people who suffer through a poor social environment; for example, when they are told about the few who are seriously adrift in most of our big cities,[5] or about those who are victims of family neglect,[6] or about those who cannot profit by educational opportunities because there is not enough knowledge or encouragement in the social class to which they belong.[7] To each of these accounts they are likely to respond by asking, 'Why don't *they* do something about it?', where 'they' equals the organized society as a whole in its provisions.

One element in the way the people of Britain think about their young is in terms of community responsibility towards them.

2   That the young are to be socialized. Human societies have drives towards self-preservation no less than individuals and pressures, both latent and manifest, are exerted upon newcomers – whether they are born into the society or migrate into it – to fit in with the existing order (at least on all matters that are deemed important) and to perpetuate the society's identity. Societies have many allies in the process of socialization – the parents and the school, for example – but one most useful ally is the individual himself who may come to internalize the values of his society and be prepared to defend them as ultimate truth. As Peter Berger has reminded us, in estimating the human situation, we have to contend not only with 'Man in Society' but also with 'Society in Man'.[8]

If we listen carefully to ourselves and others talking about youth, we can usually catch the undertones of 'socialization expectations'. We do not wish them to represent big 'cultural discontinuities', that is to break too far from what we have inherited from the past. And what is most interesting is that those of us who consider ourselves most sophisticated in our thinking on generational matters, and indeed, *avant garde*, in these matters, will in casual, unstudied remarks, betray our expectations of the socializing of the young. A man who has a reputation for discoursing on the new world which youngsters inhabit and which includes new industrial processes, technological changes, the rise of meritocracy, and the advance of urbanization, will often make a remark which shows that in an area with which he is personally and deeply concerned, he is not expecting the newcomers to challenge the old established order. People vary in the intensity with which they hold to this socialization norm – they see its application in different areas – but in general the expectation is common in the way we think about young people in Britain.

3   That the young will be 'revolutionary'. This may sound paradoxical in the light of the last section, but it is not the only area where a nation may entertain contradictory expectations. 'Revolutionary' here does not necessarily intend 'political revolutionary' though some degree of the latter is expected and tolerated.

In fact, there is a fair measure of social tolerance for the notion that 'young people are different', though the fact is discouraged from reaching dangerous consequences by the considerations described in the last paragraph. The conclusions of F. Musgrove suggest that this is not so strange, that the two attitudes belong together, that the surest way of preventing the young from over-throwing society, is to end their frustrations and give them power, when they will immediately become conservative in outlook. 'There are indications from many contrasted societies that youth will provide an impetus towards social experimentation and change not when they are given power but when they are denied it.'[9]

In discussing 'youthful rebellion', the most frequent comment we are likely to hear is that it was ever thus, that in all generations young people have had to win their spurs by staging a revolt against their elders. Audiences not necessarily composed of pro-fessional educationalists will respond quickly and intuitively to remarks and stories that illustrate the point. One example is Freud's remark that a boy does not become a man until his father dies. Another is the account of how the Black Prince was being overborne by the enemy in his first command; when news was brought to his father, the king refused to send aid and replied, 'Let the lad win his spurs.'

We, the general public in Britain, entertain 'revolutionary' expectations of our young people. So much so that the scholar quoted above, F. Musgrove, thinks that we carry this further than the facts warrant.[10]

> There is no immediate prospect of any massive rebellion by
> the young against their condition and the dominant customs,
> trends and institutions of our society. Never (at least since
> the later eighteenth century) have they given such support as
> they do today to the institution of marriage: perhaps, too,
> they were never so satisfied with the economic order and the
> jobs it offers them.

4 That the young will enjoy themselves. Finally there is a hedonistic expectation: people accept the idea that young people should have a good time. 'Enjoy yourself: you are only young once', they will say. Having more money to spend, living in a con-sumer society with many new technical devices for entertainment and at a time when it is recognized that all social classes should have equal rights to pleasure – what is more natural and inevitable than this expectation? Pop-stars are often heroes for the middle-aged too.

Several factors may be involved in this norm. It probably contains a vicarious element in several ways. One may be that the
young are enjoying the good times that the older people never had
in poorer days. Another is that older people may gain vicarious
excitement from sharing in the excitement of the young and even,
to some extent, drinking at the fountain of youth. Matza has
suggested that there is even a kind of secret alliance between the
delinquent tendencies of some teenage groups and the delinquent
tendencies of many adult people in modern societies. Fanciful as
this may sound, the popularity of crime fiction in books and on the
screen, and public sympathy for criminals who 'bring it off' like
the mail-train robbers, suggest there may be something in the view.

But these are after all speculations: what we claim as fact is the
public's 'hedonistic' expectation of the youth of Britain.

How various adult groups see young Englanders

Probably in no single adult are the four elements we have just
described evenly balanced, or to put the matter another way, perhaps no single adult is 'normal' in the sense that he represents in
his attitude exactly the same proportion of these elements as is
found in the society as a whole. Davies and Gibson have written
an amusing account of the ways in which older people may react
to adolescents in Britain if they are not sure what to make of them.[11]

> The adult [confronting a young person] finds himself in a
> state of ambiguity, receiving conflicting signals about what
> attitude he should take up ... The adult is like a baby or a
> dog faced by strange and disturbing sense impressions, and
> he reacts accordingly. He may do one of a number of things.
> He may, as it were, put his tail between his legs, or turn his
> face to the pram-pillow and so avoid the issue. Or he may try
> to propitiate the mystery by tokens of homage, by conceding
> the young person's every indicated wish and by endorsing his
> every act and attitude. Alternatively, he may try to make the
> disturbing image fit a familiar one which he knows how to
> deal with ...

To which it might be added that since few of us are consistent, each
of us attempts different 'solutions' at different times depending on
our mood or even the time of day.

But the dominant attitude to the young of any single adult will arise from a complex of reasons, having to do with personality and social experiences and circumstances. As to the first, it frequently appears as we have previously suggested, that nowhere do people tell us more about themselves – their personal philosophy, attitudes, values, convictions, prejudices – as when they talk about the young: their comments here are often a mirror held up to reflect their fear or generosity or maturity. Eysenck has suggested that our political choices are guided by our personality traits: whether we are tender-minded or tough-minded, radical or conservative, affects which party gains our support. Undoubtedly this analysis has meaning in the present discussion. And in seeking to understand adolescents today older people are tempted to project their own experience on to present realities. Again people often belong to social groups which condition their views on this matter. An enthusiast for noise abatement may hear only the roar of their motor-bikes when he contemplates the young. A strong supporter for any kind of tradition may possibly find himself not thinking too highly of the younger generation if they coolly disregard the tradition.

What are some of the common ways in which adults or groups of adults think about youth in this country? Perhaps it would be safe to say that most adopt a reasonably responsible attitude, but oft-times it is tempting to think that adult attitudes to the young have polarized in several related ways:

1 Those who stress the alienation of the young from their society. ('Alienation' has been defined as the state of feeling a stranger in your own country.)

Those who insist that the alienation of the young has been much exaggerated.

2 Those who are inclined to blame young people for their own troubles and to see them primarily as 'sinners'.

Those who blame society for the problems of young people; insist that any society gets the young people it deserves; and see them primarily as 'victims'.

3 Those who want Britain to exercise more control over its youth: Bryan Wilson writes in this vein.

Those who want the country to give more freedom and status to the young.

But perhaps it is possible to have a more detailed account. To anticipate a later stage of the argument, it will be our main contention that the most hopeful attitude that a community takes to its young is to 'expect and respect', to issue in fact constant invitations to be partners. What we are concerned with now is approaches which older people in Britain often make to younger people which are not necessarily helpful, particularly in extreme forms. And this section is related to the last in the sense that each of them are seen to be forms – often exaggerated to the point of caricature – of one of the strands of public opinion about the young.

1 That the community has a responsibility towards its youth.

a Pity. This is a common reaction and usually takes the form of judging that any juvenile problems are caused by parental neglect. Of course, as in all these cases, there is substance in the view but throughout this section we are thinking of those who allow one facet of adolescent experience, or the experience of one section of the adolescent population, to fill their whole picture.

b Patronage. This outlook may be summarized as seeing the traffic of learning and helping as able to move in one direction only – down the age structure. Figuratively, 'patting on the head' is not unknown in the relationship across the generations. A salutary meditation for educators is the last message left for his sponsors by an Arctic explorer – 'Do not rescue me prematurely.'

c Paternalism. In this, we want to care but we do not want to listen to their ideas: we think we know what is good for them. Paternalism is authoritarianism with a conscience.

d Indulgence. A spectacle which can be well observed among those parents who understand well the 'love-function' they have for their children, but do not grasp that they also have a 'truth-function'. In other words, they can give them the security of an unchanging affection but do not provide the firmness or encourage the self-discipline which will enable the children to face their own life-tasks.

e Service. Obviously, we are not thinking here of the laudable motive that lies behind the acceptance of educational responsibility, in the widest sense, for younger members of the community. Again, we are thinking of this in its distorted or exaggerated forms when the young are seen almost entirely defined as 'those to be served'. There are parents who sacrifice themselves so completely for their children, that they virtually cease to have 'any life apart from them'. There are some youth workers who have developed an urgent psychological need to be serving young people.

Of these first five views an inclusive criticism is that they assign a too passive role to the young.

2   That the young are to be socialized.

a Indoctrination. Here in most cases the adult has a commitment to a value system; it may be religious, political or an activity like drama, boxing or mountain-climbing. The universal factor is that he projects his own experience on to the youngster; he gratuitously assumes that what was determinative for him will be determinative for others. 'Boxing will make a man of him because boxing made a man of me.' In the worst cases the enthusiast divides the human race neatly into two – those who support his commitment and those who do not.

b Recruitment. This is the organizational aspect of the last view: it is the attempt to gather juvenile members of the movements which express the ideological commitment – church, political party, hobby, reforming or special interest structure. Many traditional movements at their reviews show their awareness of the reality that they cannot survive without recruitment from the new generation.

c Condemnation. Not uncommonly there are expressions of opinion which lump all the members of one age-group together and judge them to be unsatisfactory.

d Fear. This is the last approach carried further. It sees the young as enemies. In excess, they are scapegoats and they have of course the characteristics of scapegoats – they are visually identifiable by their hair and dress styles and they tend to congregate together. Where the young are seen primarily in terms of threat, there usually follow demands for their more effective social control.

The prevailing unsatisfactory constituent of these four attitudes is that they underestimate the degree of change in our country; they are too prone to expect the newcomers to accept what they find uncritically.

3   That the young will be 'revolutionary'.

a Emancipation. An interpretation which is found more commonly among professional educationalists and sociologists though it is far from being universal among them. Its basic tenets are that older people are mistaken in supposing that they know enough to give complete guidance to the young, that they culpably use their positions of power to restrict the spontaneity of youth. They perpetuate traditions no longer appropriate in the New Age; they deny the recognition of adult status and even 'invent adolescence'.

b Imitation. The newcomers are depicted as the trend-setters who are pioneering a new style of living and are to be copied by all those with courage and initiative. The phenomenon of 'adult teenagers' is not unknown.

c Appointment to lead a social and political revolution. This is the last emphasis carried to positive, activist and political lengths. Some adults nourish strong expectations that a new quality of community life will emerge from the idealism and activities of the young who can see more clearly than the rest of us that cynicism, materialism, insincerity, greed and dishonesty are crushing the human spirit.

The fallacy behind these three interpretations is that they may exaggerate the disposition and ability of the young to effect radical change: young people are probably on the whole more conservative in outlook than those enthusiasts think. It has been said, for example, that the task of persuading the conformist majority of young Englanders to react with more idealism and adventure to life is bigger than the problem of persuading the alienated minority to be less destructive and anti-social. The optimistic view expressed above may not come to terms with the reality that the 'revolutionary idealism' of youth is the radicalism of those who carry little social responsibility.

4 That the young will enjoy themselves.

a Envy. There are older people in Britain whose dominant feeling about the young – though often unacknowledged – is jealousy, and this not only because they see them as in possession of the incomparable, though wasting assets, which they have lost – energy, strength, freedom, opportunity, beauty – but also because the general conditions of life are so much better for the new generation.

b A source of vicarious excitement, entertainment and enjoyment. 'I like to see young people enjoying themselves', means I am

7

also enjoying myself in their enjoyment. This feature dominates the way some older people think of and approach youth. As we have seen, Matza believes that there is a secret understanding between juvenile delinquents and the delinquent sympathies of the whole population.[12]

Both these adult groups are liable to the misjudgment that 'the grass is always greener on your neighbour's lawn': they seriously undervalue the problems of being young in a complex society like ours.

Like other categories, these are incomplete: their features overlap: they describe the common characteristics of groups of adults rather than the unique features of one adult, but they are an attempt to introduce some order into the mass of evidence at our disposal.

How young Englanders see themselves

Here we are concerned to discover how the young Englanders identify themselves for their society, not always by their self-consciousness but by their behaviour. And this is perhaps the first general and qualifying statement to make. It is not suggested that the young exist in a continual state of awareness of being young. Like other marginal and minority groups in the country, for example, 'immigrants', one guesses that they desire two kinds of association: one when they are mixing with others of their 'kind', in this case members of the same age group as themselves; and another when they are not distinguished from the rest of the community. There is a good deal of private resentment among them when adolescents are written about and spoken about as though they were a different breed. As long ago as 1960 the Albemarle Report said, 'It is not surprising, then that young people to-day are often unusually self-conscious. They know they are much talked about.'[13] They sense there is something wrong when older people identify them too exclusively by their age.

On the other hand it is probably true that for various reasons other than public interest there is, in comparison with previous eras, a heightened awareness of being different from others because one is young, in fact, of a wider 'generation gap'. We have already examined the reasons in the discussions about teenage spending power, the growth of pop culture and the general features of rapid social change. There are certainly important areas in which it is common for young people to feel that adult guidance and judgment is no longer adequate.

This leads naturally to the central consideration of the subject of the self-identification of the young in relation to the whole community: how widespread and how deep is the feeling of alienation? Careful investigation has modified extremist views which suggest that there is widespread and serious rejection by young people of the values of their society. Let E. M. and E. Eppel speak for several. In concluding their study of the moral attitudes of young working people they write: 'There is indeed evidence of a change in some respects of their moral codes and sentiments but it involves a shift in emphasis and focus and a re-evaluation of the sanctions for moral conduct rather than an adoption of a completely new set of principles or the approbation of radically different forms of conduct.'[14] The same quotation suggests that we may on the contrary underestimate how far young people have rejected the norms of their society. Not unknown is the assertion that any social criticism and any social deviation is restricted to a minority of young people and to students. What this view overlooks is the possibility that this articulate minority may to some extent be the tip of an iceberg of adolescent dissent. To this point we return later in greater detail.

If on this subject we wish to create the kind of categories that we had in the two previous related subjects, then it is to the notion of 'alienation' that we look as a main principle of division. Thus, one simple typology is (a) The conformists, (b) The experimenters, and (c) the desocialized. This has the merit of being brief. It also manages to convey a distinction between two kinds of young people who do not fit in with things as they find them: the experimenters, might in fact be called 'the socially-rejecting' as they usually want to change society; the desocialized on the other hand are usually the 'socially-rejected' in the sense that they are usually characterized by deprivation. But despite these merits the scheme suffers from lack of detail and as a consequence puts together in the same category youngsters whose dominant attitudes are demonstrably different.

One typology has been provided by J. B. Mays.[15] The following is a summary of it.

Group 1 This group comprises those youngsters who react with hostility against frustrating environmental circumstances.

Group 2 This group is made up of youngsters who are similarly socially depressed and unsuccessful but who do not react to their frustration and denigration by open hostility and aggression against respectable law-abiding sections of the community.

Group 3 This group consists of the more thoughtful and intellectually and morally committed young people irrespective of social class background. They are the latter-day Angry Young Men.

Group 4 This is a smaller and deviant section of the youthful population who reject the contemporary world and along with it almost everything else.

Group 5 These are the new men and women of the affluent society, for the most part working class or lower middle class in origin but viewing the world around them confidently and even a little pugnaciously.

Group 6 This is made up of those middle-class, grammar and public-school battalions who have made a good adjustment to their own favourable background and who have sufficient ability to get on well in the milieux of professional, business and commercial life.

Under pressure of criticism, Professor Mays added a seventh group: those who are less able than the average, who are almost by definition lower class but who are well adjusted to their station in life and accept their lowly status with equanimity – the contented proletarian base, in fact, who have no urge to rebel.

Michael Carter provides an interesting typology of young workers in terms of the varying kinds of 'home and social background' from which they come.[16]

1 The home-centred aspiring family. Independence and respectability are the keynotes in these families. There is a desire to maintain standards and give the children a good opportunity in life: parents take an interest in schools' events and encourage their offspring to join churches and youth organizations. There are two sub-divisions of this category – the traditional respectable family and the newly affluent, but they both tend to 'produce' the same kind of youngster – aspiring, respectful to various forms of authority and concerned with appearances.

2   The solid working-class type which is distinguishable from the first type by a lesser concern with 'appearances' and 'getting on', and by a tendency to accept life as it comes. They do not expect a lot out of life and they take their pleasures, as their sorrows, with some equanimity. The children know they can rely upon their parents for general encouragement and do not feel held down, but they do not expect their parents to be able to give them expert guidance about the world of work.

3   The rough deprived underprivileged type of home and family background where there is little regard for the 'official' norms and values of society. Parents live for the present, spending money quickly as soon as they get it: repudiate the values of the school and have as little to do with them as possible: do not encourage their children to join 'official' youth organizations, which in their view are full of snobs. Where they ask does 'honesty' come in – is not 'dishonesty' rife everywhere? Life is a matter of luck – but you don't get much luck if you are not ready to take a chance when it comes along. From these homes come many 'deprived' young-sters who are ill-equipped but ready-made for 'dead-end' jobs and anti-social in their behaviour.

Our categories offered here are based on a main division be-tween those whose dominant attitudes to life, the society in which they find themselves and their place in it seems to be one of con-tent – the assenters, and those whose dominant attitude seems to be one of discontent – the dissenters. The second group is here divided into two sub-divisions: first, those who are usually seen to be discontented with society as they find it and want to effect revolutionary changes; and second, those who are conspicuously discontented with their personal fate in the scheme of things. We have already identified these two groups as the 'socially-rejecting' and the 'socially-rejected'. One or two general comments may be useful before entering into details. To repeat a previous cautionary word – none of these categories pretend to describe completely a single adolescent. Moreover, they do not represent completely water-tight divisions and they involve hard decisions about par-ticular social acts: certain behaviour can be interpreted in one of several ways depending on the life style of the individual and his inner intention. Thus, drug-addiction can conceivably be a form of escapism or a revolutionary gesture. So the categories at certain points tend to 'run into one another'. And it is interesting to

observe that there was at least one incident in the story of international youth when two related attitudes were found to be in the
sharpest conflict when it had been assumed that they could be
harmonized.

In the spring of 1967, at the great San Francisco protest parade
against the Vietnam War, an attempt was made to unite in common
action the political radicals, concerned to change the world, with
the hippies, concerned to enjoy life more. The hippies enjoyed the
procession more than the speeches. When the radicals accused
them of having wrecked a solemn occasion with their levity and
loose behaviour, the hippy retort was, 'Well, why let Vietnam give
you a bum day?'[17]

The last comment is that the following list represents, among
many others, a conviction that the 'socially-rejected',cannot simply
be equated with the 'deprived'. There are, as we saw in May's
seventh group, those youngsters who in the judgment of the observer, are deprived but are not significant for their discontent;
their lot is a poor one but they seem happy enough with it.
Whereas the category of 'socially-rejected' is reserved for those
who are manifestly and significantly aware of their deprivations,
resent them and react to them in discernible ways. There is at least
one perceptive and sympathetic observer of the adolescent scene
whose careful researches have suggested to him that the spread of
a sense of failure and rejection among the less favoured youngsters,
at least in the educational realm, has been grossly exaggerated.[18]

There is an idea which has widespread credence, that to-day,
quite apart from question of birth, our educational system
selects a 'privileged' – or anyway a highly favoured – minority
and leaves the great bulk of young people with a sense of
failure, rejection and resentment . . . The psychological tests
which were devised to compare the way in which 'selected'
and 'unselected' adolescents saw themselves and their society
showed conflicts among grammar-school pupils which would
scarcely be expected among a favoured, high-status minority.
Far from feeling at one with a beneficent world, they
appeared beset by irreconcilable social demands. The
'rejected', the 'failures' in the modern schools, seemed to suffer
far less doubt and uncertainty, and to identify themselves far
more closely with the adult world.

Typology of young Englanders

1   *The 'assenters', the 'content', the conformists*

The majority of young people are to be found in this group. There may be fringes of rebellion in their attitudes, but basically they go along with things as they are whilst thus peripherally fulfilling the 'revolutionary' expectations of the older members of their society; most youngsters for example, even after a possible phase of delinquency, grow up to marry, go out to work and keep the law to the level of 'average' behaviour in this matter. Anybody who doubts this should initiate conversation on public issues of the day among groups of young people and see how faithfully their contributions reflect the commonly held views on these subjects. It has even been suggested that the stolid respectability of the majority is frightening in the sense of Tawney's dictum that 'the first duty of youth is not to avoid mistakes, but to show initiative and take responsibility, to make a tradition, not to perpetuate one'.

But not all the 'assenters' are the same and among them we may identify the following types at least:

a The privileged who are content mainly to accept their privileges. From the beginning they seem marked out to be the darlings of fate: they come from homes of at least comparative wealth; the doors of educational opportunity are opened for them; they are surrounded with love and care and encouragement; more and more in a technical age like ours, they must succeed by their own efforts but every circumstance of their social environment builds up their self-confidence to succeed. Their usual path is public school, older universities and one of the professions. They appear to be untroubled by the thought that life might be unfair in giving so much to them and depriving others.

b The unreflecting conformists. They are found in every social class and are not confined to the privileged. It simply never seems to occur to them to be dissatisfied with any aspects of their society or their own place in it. This is often because of the intense reality of their own private world, filled with music or art, or merely their own private thoughts, but sometimes it appears that youngsters in this category simply lack the intellectual initiative to question what is given to them.

c The 'ritualists' is a title which describes those youngsters who are not uncritical of many features of their society and of their own place in it.[19] Indeed, they may often indulge in conversations where they reveal an impressive knowledge of the defects of life, but their attitudes are not fundamentally affected by this awareness. In other words, they are agreed 'to work the system': they have settled for a quiet life. Depending on our general view we may accuse them of 'bad faith' in the sense that Sartre applies this term to those who, say, like a judge who does not believe in capital punishment still sentences a murderer to death: they say that they cannot help themselves, or they may say that most individuals have minimal influence to affect 'things as they are'.

d The strivers. We are thinking of those youngsters – usually from working-class or lower middle-class homes – who lift themselves up the social ladder by strenuous efforts in full-time or part-time education. Since they are dissenters in the sense that they are seeking to change their position, it may be surprising to find them under the general heading of the conformists. But this is justified on the grounds that their dominant attitude is one of acceptance of life as they find it. They are not usually found grumbling except perhaps occasionally when they observe that jobs and promotion go unfairly with the right accent and public-school background. In fact, the opportunities of a meritocratic society suit them well. John Braine's Joe Lampton is a good example.

e The hedonists. Others are satisfied because a modern society like ours gives plenty of opportunity for pleasure and excitement commercially provided. This group is to be distinguished from another group, a prominent feature of whose use of pleasure is escape from life-tasks which are too threatening. This latter group is a later concern. The distinction is a fine one but at least theoretically it can be made. It is conceivable that at an early stage at least youngsters use 'soft' drugs primarily for a new pleasurable experience and that some youngsters are using drugs as a means of escape into a world of illusion.

2   *The experimenters*

This general category covers those who dislike and reject their society and/or their place in it but who make a 'positive' response to their discontent by supporting new systems for human associations or for individual styles of life. Of course, this attitude normally requires a degree of confidence and that is why it is found more frequently among students whose selection for higher education bolsters their self-confidence.

There are other general features of the experimenters. The movement has its internationally recognized Messiahs, like, in some sections, Che Guevara, its philosopher-kings like Marcuse, its pop-idols like Mick Jagger. It tends to be Leftish in political sympathies. It depends upon an international network of communication. Youth protest songs are sung in many lands. Activist leaders of the experimenters move from country to country.

We suggest below that there are two sub-divisions of the experimenters. The first consists of those whose main effort is devoted to changing their society. The second is those who strive above all to create for themselves and others who will join them, a new style of life usually based on protest against bureaucratic concepts of behaviour and the right 'to do one's own thing' and to pursue a private version of the pleasurable.

These next divisions conceal wide disparities of intensity of commitment to the 'revolution'. At one entrance are those who seem obsessional about their programme and see everything else through the spectacles of 'revolution' and subordinate every other consideration to its claims. By contrast, there are those who are willing to play the game whilst inwardly admitting to themselves that it is a game. Peer expectations may pressurize them into giving assent to revolutionary views among their contemporaries, but they are not totally committed. And one suspects that 'when the chips are down', they will join the reactionaries. Hence, nobody knows how large is the body of 'experimenters' among the youth population. Perhaps the majority of their generation are attracted by the philosophy of the movement but certainly there are many camp-followers.

A The political revolutionaries There are many varieties. Perhaps we can identify one or two general features. It is a minority movement, even among students[20] who are the largest proportion of the adherents, though its underlying philosophy affects a much wider constituency. It is fragmented, with a history of many internal quarrels: indeed it is tempting to think that its history is a commentary on the text 'revolutions do not last for long'.[21] It has strong Marxist sympathies (though not necessarily with historical and contemporary forms of Communism) and believes that capitalism and materialism are crushing the human spirit: for many of these revolutionaries, Marxism has replaced Christianity as a moral frame of reference. This is one point at which the generation gap is wide: it is unusual to find adults who appreciate the degree of alienation of these young people from their society or the strength, consistency and, to them, satisfying logic of their position. They are likely to believe, for example, that governments are more immoral than the worst criminals; that the power of the ballot-box is a mirage; that many forms of social control are a conspiracy; that there can be no human freedom until the ruling classes are overthrown. The break in communication may also be traced to the inflexibility with which these views are held and expressed by the extremists. The philosophy then becomes absolutely true and anybody who disagrees is dishonest and insincere. It becomes a secular equivalent of the more pessimistic versions of the Christian doctrine of Original Sin. Anybody who disagrees is fighting against the truth but is, in fact, demonstrating the truth by their opposition since this is what the doctrine predicts.

These are the general features. The following is an attempt to supply a typology of political revolutionaries in a 'descending scale of alienation'.

a The individualists. They are not a coherent group and it is hard to see what they are after: anarchistic and nihilistic, usually ready to use violence, they want to destroy present society but it is not clear what they wish to put in its place.

b Orthodox Marxists. They also do not eschew violence.

c The New Left. They are chiefly distinguished from (b) by their rejection of Soviet Communism which they do not regard as a workers' democracy.

d The demonstrators. This title is intended to describe those who have no strong party affiliations but who are ready to march on particular issues.

e Students' rights protesters. They are far more likely to be active for students' participation and status than for general issues of race, peace and war and social injustice, though they use these general issues to support their case.

f New party advocates. They wish to create new political structures or new political parties or change one of the old parties out

of recognition. Some of the Young Liberals are a good example.
g The traditionalists. They join one of the traditional parties as offering opportunities for change.
h The discriminators. They approve some things in their society though they may want to change others quite profoundly, but always by non-violent constitutional methods. They tend to gravitate into community work where they are concerned to help citizens to know and gain their rights as well as extend those rights. They recognize the need for personal service as well as political action.

B The 'personal' revolutionaries The heading here is intended to designate those who are seeking a new way of life, but not so much for a whole society: their focus of attention is on a new style of life for themselves and their friends and contemporaries. They are often identified by older people as 'drop-outs' and are considered to have taken all the benefits of their culture but to have accepted none of the responsibilities it lays upon them. There are at least three strands of this attitude which cannot be disentangled in order to make three sub-groups. There is the hedonistic strand – 'have a good time, the rest is propaganda'. There is the fellowship strand as in some of the 'communes' where an attempt is made to develop new forms of social relationships. There is the anarchist strand (linking this with (a) in the last main category) where there is present a protest at the notion that the society should in any way interfere with the freedom of the individual.

3 *The deprived, desocialized, 'socially-rejected'*

What happens to young people in Britain who feel they have been let down by their society or by significant adults in their experience, to whom a message has been flashed, though not explicitly, that they are second-class citizens? The considered judgment of many researchers is that there is a large group of youngsters in Britain whose dominant feelings about the community is that it has failed them, treated them unfairly in comparison with others. 'They are denigrated by the social system, made to feel inferior at every stage of their development, and allotted a place at or near the base of the social pile' (J. B. Mays).[22] 'Success is closed to most teenagers once they are committed to the secondary modern school, except by a win on the pools or by sudden "stardom" '

(Bryan Wilson).[23] '. . . adequate education in slum areas will always be expensive, more expensive than average. It looks to us as if it has often been less expensive than average, and therefore pitifully inadequate. It is time for a change' (Newsom Report).[24]

How any young person will respond to an inner feeling of deprivation will depend upon a number of factors including his own character, his home, family and neighbourhood background, the quality and atmosphere of the school he attends, the possible encounter with influential adults, the friendships he forms and fortuitous circumstances. Among the 'socially-rejected' we suggest the following groups may be identified by their dominant responses:

a The stars. This is a very small group who are discovered to have an outstanding talent in sport or entertainment, who rise rapidly to the top and become objects of envy and adulation for millions in the same age-group.

b The self-educators. Compared with the first group immediately above, they have average talents, but by strenuous efforts they lift themselves above their depressing circumstances. They succeed, against the odds, which they resent and they know it: they are the 'self-made' men.

c The disgruntled. These are characterized by a willingness to join in 'mildly' anti-social acts which stop short of serious crime or destruction. Part of their motivation is to work out a grudge.

d The delinquents. Delinquency is one of those subjects which shows itself to be more complex the more closely one examines it, but internationally two related features have often been found to be recurring. One is that delinquency has the highest incidence among that section of the youth population who are not very clever and hence will not receive the rewards of a meritocratic society: hence it is believed that they are seeking prestige, identity, significance and status through delinquent acts. The other is that delinquent attitudes are often found in association with a sense of grievance: part of their motivation is to 'get their own back'.

e The hooligans and vandals. These show many of the characteristics of the last group but their distinguishing mark is that they make no personal gain from their delinquent acts: it is destruction for destruction's own sake rather than theft. Probably the grudge is felt more strongly and the response to it is more active.

45791

f The members of identifiable peer groups like Hell's Angels and Skinheads, who are not simply to be put in (c) (d) or (e) since though their attitudes may include elements of an anti-social and delinquent nature, this is not the whole picture nor is it true of all the members of these groups.

g The escapists. They are using some kind of 'drug' to escape from the harsh realities of their human situation. It may literally be drugs but it may be the use of the world of entertainment and sport as a fantasy into which to retreat. (Nearly ten years ago, the Cuban crisis was one of the few international political events which penetrated the protective covering of this group: they felt seriously threatened. But when the crisis had passed they quickly slipped back into their dreams.)

h The privatists. They only differ from the last group in the sense that the 'world' into which they retreat contains more continuing challenges of excellence and achievement. We are clearly not thinking merely of educational enthusiasms – like drama, athletics, art – but only of those cases where this enthusiasm is carried to the point of being compulsively necessary to the youngster for personal significance. (Difficult to distinguish of course from the 'hedonists'.)

i The drifters. They are those who make a negative dispirited response to their deprivation: they are at the mercy of circumstance and seem to have little energy even for wrongdoing. Every major city has probably a small group of serious cases of drifters.

j The 'shilly-shallyers'. Members of this group are distinguished from the last by being more active. They are capable of enjoying more, particularly in pop-culture, but they are one thing today and another tomorrow; their responses have little consistency; they appear to be having more than average difficulty in establishing a reasonably stable self-image which is one of the life-tasks of adolescence.

k The 'can-copes'. We must not forget what is probably the largest group among the 'socially-rejected' – those who realize that in comparison with many other young people in Britain, they have been deprived. They do not become 'swots', anxious social risers, but they overcome their difficulties to some extent, make something of life and, despite even a possible period of juvenile delinquency, grow up to be respectable citizens, workers and parents.

This analysis of the social position of young Englanders has brought us to the threshold of the last chapter in which we hope to explain in more detail the underlying point of view of the present work, and indeed to offer a few practical suggestions for more hopeful relationships between youth on the one hand and the whole community and older people on the other, though we would want hastily to disclaim any competence to show how the approach we approve can apply to more than a few limited areas.

The connecting link then between this chapter and the next is a list of brief statements which seek to cut across the earlier definitions of the present chapter and prepare the way for a fuller discussion of the relationships which the whole community should encourage with youth.

1   Respect and expect. They are 'their own people' (compare the incident in the life of Osborne's Luther when he realizes that his son does not belong to him but to God); yet in another profound sense, they 'belong to the community'.

2   Invite them to be active – not sleeping – partners in a social enterprise. They are there to define national goals as well as to share them. The best thing a society ever says to its young is 'come over and help us'.

3   Older people should neither patronize nor indulge young people. Pats on the head are insulting to the young, degrading and humiliating. They should be challenged, but not with a tradition which has no credentials except history, but with excellence which can be trusted to speak for itself. The past can often enrich them: it should never enslave them.

4   Older people must learn how to care for the young without being fussy.

5   Older people must listen carefully to what they have to say, take it seriously into account, try to discover the common goals which could make us a more civilized community, but they must not be afraid to express their own views at the right time.

Notes

1   Bernard D. Davies and Alan Gibson, *The Social Education of the Adolescent*, University of London Press, 1967, pp. 50, 52.

2   The reader wishing to pursue this line of thought should read C. M. Fleming, *Adolescence: its Social Psychology*, Routledge & Kegan Paul, 1963.

3 By contrast compare the methods and the writings of one
  investigator, F. Zweig, who respects his interviewees, listens
  to them and tries to gain a full picture. A good example is
  The Quest for Fellowship, Heinemann, 1965.
4 Cf. *Community Work and Social Change. A Report on Training*,
  Gulbenkian Foundation, Longmans, 1968.
5 *Rootless in Cities*, N.C.S.S., 1967.
6 Cf. A. Clegg & B. Megson, *Children in Distress*, Penguin Books.
7 B. Jackson & D. Marsden, *Education and the Working Class*,
  Penguin Books.
8 Cf. Peter Berger, *Invitation to Sociology*, Penguin Books.
9 F. Musgrove, *Youth and the Social Order*, Routledge & Kegan
  Paul, 1964, p. 3.
10 Ibid., p. 19.
11 Op. cit., p. 72.
12 David Matza, 'Subterranean traditions of youth' in *Annals of the
  American Academy of Political & Social Science*, November 1961,
  pp. 102–18.
13 Ministry of Education, *The Youth Service in England & Wales*
  (Albemarle Report), HMSO, 1960, paragraph 121.
14 E. M. and M. Eppel, *Adolescents & Morality*, Routledge &
  Kegan Paul, 1966, p. 213. For the same point demonstrated in
  relation to sexual ethics, cf. M. Schofield, *The Sexual Behaviour
  of Young People*, Longmans, 1965, and with reference to relationships between older adults and adolescents, cf. F. Musgrove,
  op. cit.
15 I. Bulman, M. Craft & F. Milson (eds), *Youth Service and Inter-
  professional Studies*, Pergamon Press, 1970.
  Chapter I, 'Young People in Contemporary British Society',
  J. B. Mays.
16 Cf. Michael Carter, *Into Work*, Penguin Books, pp. 40ff.
17 Reported in Bryan Wilson's *The Youth Culture and the
  Universities*, Faber, 1970, p. 201.
18 F. Musgrove, op. cit., p. 3.
19 The title in fact is borrowed from a description by R. K. Merton
  of the five individual personality types which develop in a
  society which offers socially-acceptable goals for all but does
  not offer to all socially-acceptable means of achieving those
  goals. Cf. R. K. Merton, *Social Theory and Social Structure*.

20   'Although student movements reflect unintended consequences
      of the nature and expansion of higher education. . . . student
      protest is chiefly a reflection of conflicts of values, generated
      intentionally or unintentionally by their education. Students

have the time and the intellectual inclination to attend to the
politics of their country. They are one of the few social groups
available for political action. Characteristically, students have
few family or financial responsibilities. They risk less than
other social groups in espousing courses hostile to the
established interests of their society.'
Introducing Sociology, Peter Worsley (ed.), Penguin Books, p. 176.

21 The point is well illustrated in the history of the troubles at the
London School of Economics as recorded by Colin Crouch in
Student Revolt, Bodley Head, 1970, Part I. From this account
one could be forgiven for concluding that a wise strategy of the
authorities would have been not to oppose too strongly since the
movement would destroy itself!

22 Op. cit., p. 7.

23 Op. cit., p. 28.

24 *Half our Future* (Newsom Report), Central Advisory Council for
Education (England), HMSO, 1963.

Suggestions for further reading

General works on the social position of young people in Britain

Eppel, E. M. & E., *Adolescents and Morality*, Routledge & Kegan
Paul, 1966.

Gorer, G., 'Teenage Morals', symposium published by *Education*,
1961.

Klein, J., *Samples from English Culture*, Routledge & Kegan Paul,
1965.

Musgrove, F., *Youth and the Social Order*, Routledge & Kegan
Paul, 1964.

Schofield, M., *The Sexual Behaviour of Young People*, Longmans,
1965.

Smith, Cyril S., *Adolescence*, Longmans, 1968.

Willmott, P. *Adolescent Boys in East London*, Routledge & Kegan
Paul, 1966.

Bryan Wilson, 'The social content of the youth problem',
Thirteenth Charles Russell Lecture, 1966.

Adult attitudes to the young in Britain

Musgrove, F., op. cit., chapters 2, 3, 5.

Report of the Committee on the Age of Majority (Latey Report),
HMSO, 1967.

Wilson, Bryan, *The Youth Culture and the Universities*, Faber, 1970.

Different social groups of young Englanders

Anderson, R. & Blackburn R. (eds), *Towards Socialism*, Collins, 1965.

Beckett, Dale, 'Should we legalize pot?', *New Society*, 18 May 1967.

Bland, Mary, *Razor Edge – The Study of a Youth Club*, Gollancz, 1967.

Carter, M. P., *Into Work*, Penguin Books.

Crouch, Colin, *The Student Revolt*, Bodley Head, 1970.

Fyvel, T. R., *The Insecure Offenders*, Penguin Books.

Goetschius, G., & Tash, J., *Working with Unattached Youth*, Routledge & Kegan Paul, 1967.

Harms, Ernest (ed.), *Drug Addiction in Youth*, Pergamon Press, 1965

Hudson, Jan, *Hell's Angels*, New English Library, 1967. (Though this is about the USA there is nothing comparable for Britain)

Jephcot, Pearl, *Some Young People*, Allen & Unwin, 1954.

Jones, Howard, *Crime in a Changing Society*, Penguin Books.

Jordan, Brenda & Leech, Kenneth, *Drugs for Young People*, Pergamon Press, 1968.

Mays, J. B., *Education and the Urban Child*, Liverpool University Press, 1962.

Morse, Mary, *The Unattached*, Penguin Books.

Musgrove, F., op. cit., chapter 6.

N.A.Y.C., *Industrial Youth Project*, 1968.

Partridge, John, *Life in a Secondary Modern School*, Penguin Books.

Salisbury, Harrison, *The Shook-up Generation*, Michael Joseph, 1959.

West, D. J., *The Young Offenders*, Penguin Books.

Wilson, Bryan, op. cit., chapters 2, 8, 13.

Woolfe, R., 'Young people and trade unions', *Youth Review*, No. 6, June 1966.

Young C., *Educating the Intelligent*, Penguin Books.

8

5 Education for democracy

It is best to begin by defining our terms, though this may involve the repetition of one or two points made in earlier chapters.

'Democracy' must be one of the others words that the poet W. H. Auden had in mind when he wrote:

All words like peace and love,
All sane affirmative speech
Has been soiled, profaned, debased
To a horrid mechanical screech.

'Democracy' is used to describe and justify different, and in important respects, contrasting, systems of government on both sides of the 'Iron Curtain'. In common speech it – or its derivatives – are used in a humorous or even satirical sense. 'I suppose that's the price we pay for democracy.' 'We can't be too democratic.'

We cannot simply say that a 'democratic country' is one where the political representatives are elected by secret ballot or where the voter can choose a candidate from more than one party. Again, this description would serve to describe countries with opposing political systems. Democratic machinery does not in fact guarantee the democratic process anywhere.

We choose to use the word here to describe the political organization of a country first in a way that satisfies a minimum requirement, namely, that the government of the day and their basic political philosophies can be discussed, criticized and replaced, that there is open discussion not of this or that measure or appointment but of the total outlook of the ruling power. We have immediately to blunt the definition by saying that this freedom will stop short of lawbreaking, of threat to life and property and institutions, and of course many of the current controversies in 'Western democracies' revolve around the issue of what is sabotage and what is democratic expression of public feeling, and the 'Western democracies' sometimes face the dilemma of whether they will allow democratic machinery to be used to destroy the democratic intention. Despite these qualifications, it is the present view that enough is left to be a definition: that whatever substance there may be in the strictures of extreme Left-wing revolutionaries, 'democracy' has a meaning in Britain that it does not carry say in the German Democratic Republic (East Germany) or in Czechoslovakia.

But so far we have described the minimal requirement of the definition. At a more positive, generous and liberal level it means for us a society where all feasible opportunities are taken to spread power among the people. It means, in fact, the application to a national group of what Etzioni has called 'the active society'.[1] 'Democracy' for us then, in this discussion, does not stop short at the ballot-box and the multi-party system, nor even at the power of the electorate to change their political rulers and reject their policies, but it reaches out to the notion that our 'society' should always be on the look-out for areas where the citizens can be democratically involved in decision making.

This is the central notion which lies behind all the fine talk in recent years about 'participation' and 'community development'.[2] Many people regard this way of thinking as foolish, optimistic, dangerous and nonsensical. They point out that most people in this country do not want to 'participate' – they merely want to be left alone to live their private lives – and they point to the poor response that they make when given the chance to vote on specific issues, like the Manchester issue about whether the Corporation should run a lottery to support public funds. In reply, it might be argued that people may not seize on opportunities for participation because on those kinds of issues the experience is novel; just as many coloured slaves in the Deep South fulfilled racist prophecies about themselves, by 'misusing' their freedom after emancipation. Moreover, the 'community developers' are usually found to be talking about opportunities being offered to those who do want to 'participate'.

But it is not the present intention to argue the pros and cons of community development: the general validity of that case is here largely assumed. People are more likely on the whole to support those decisions in which they have had a hand and thus individual responsibility for what happens increases at a crucial time of growth of population and urbanization. Many of the old bureaucratic structures of power in this country are no longer appropriate for an educated populace. A participant society stands more chance of being responsive to necessary social changes, indeed such a society will facilitate necessary social change. Community development as previously defined appears to be required at the present time, not only to up-date the democratic process, but to satisfy the need of many people to feel that they belong to a community at a time when many natural social groupings are breaking up. Moreover, the planners whose vast schemes affect the lives of hundreds of thousands should be aware of the total needs of human beings, including the need of many for a sense of community: there are times when it is possible and desirable to ask people to define those needs themselves.

This inadequate excursion into the realms of the 'active society' is intended only to prepare for a last concentration on the subject of young Englanders at a time of rapid social change. One large purpose of Britain with its youth should be to educate them for democracy in the two senses in which it has been defined, not forgetting the second far more formidable part, namely to offer them opportunities for community involvement, responsibility, participation and decision-making. The 'Western democracies' are weakened by their failure to teach social responsibility to the young (though, as we shall see presently the phrase requires careful definition) and this also represents a loss for many of the young people themselves since it makes it more difficult for them to achieve identity and significance. 'The Soviet system suggests that to make the school an integral part of the political and economic structure and to give youth a productive role, central planning of the whole economy is necessary. Whether or not a democratic state can achieve such planning is a profound question. Apparently, however, it must either achieve it or go out of existence.'[3]

In the later sections of this final chapter an attempt will be made to indicate the growing points for a relationship between youth and the rest of the community that might help to improve the quality of life for all of us in Britain, not to terminate any conflict between the generations, but to use the conflict for social progress. But it would be quite wrong to hint that there is a panacea for intergenerational strife and misunderstanding or that a few simple measures will produce the instant mature society. Whatever may be wrong with the social position of youth in Britain, part of the trouble lies deeply embedded in the attitudes of human beings, on both sides of the generational fence. And changing attitudes, as we know, is usually a long and often a painful process.

The standpoint of the present work may be re-stated briefly. In their approaches to the young, modern societies should include a strong element of what is best described as 'permission and support and a genuine cry for help'. It is the latter aspect which is most conspicuously absent: and therefore our concentration will be on this aspect. Any reader who doubts this judgment should test it by a little homework. Study one week's newspapers or one week's television programmes from the point of view of their frequent attitudes to youth. At their worst these presentations say uncritically 'Aren't they lovely?' or 'Aren't they awful?' At a more responsible level they show the young as in need of freedom and care. Only rarely are they shown as partners in running a country as a human society, called in these days of change, to define the tasks as well as to share them.

Though regimentation is always an evil it does not follow that *laissez-faire* is always good: it can lead to aimlessness and feelings of inferiority.

There are many reasons of course why there are not more frequent examples of this kind of communication between the generations. Not least is the reason that conversation involves listening as well as talking. Sometimes we see comic episodes on the television screen where the point of the joke is that two people are talking to each other but as each one speaks in turn, it is clear that he is pursuing his own line of thought unaffected by what the other has just said. In many places today that seems to be true of conversations between older and younger people: they are not listening to – though they may be hearing – what the other is saying.

Many factors may inhibit 'conversation': let us name a few. The young may bring to the encounter a rigid dogmatism, say, that all organized activity in a society is part of a vast capitalist conspiracy. In that case, older people in authority will find it hard to do the right thing for them and everything they do will be regarded with suspicion. In 1968 the Select Committee of Education of the House of Commons visited universities to study the root causes of student revolt. Radical students saw this as a further attempt at interference and in some places the committee had a stormy reception. Adults may not be listening for a variety of reasons. They too may be deafened by their own dogmatisms and wonder why the young will not turn to what are, for the old, patently the true values, or they may see change always as a threat and never a stimulating challenge, or they may simply not realize that times have changed and that 'the transition from discipline by order and conventions to self-discipline is not easy in any field':[4] or they may simply have lost confidence in their right and ability to guide or challenge the young at any point of their experience.[5]

Listening across the generations requires the abandonment of infallible assumptions of one's own views, a willingness to learn and some confidence, but perhaps most of all it requires the sharing of tasks. A group of people who are drawn together by a common interest, or activity, or social goal, find that the differences in age among those taking part are not usually very important. This is true when the common interest is cultural – an activity with a clear achievement like the production of a play or a concert. Where the object is 'moral', that is where the goal carries features of a fight for right and justice and truth, the unity between the generations appears to be more noticeable. So the traffic travels both ways: when younger and older members of a community listen to each other they are more likely to discover common moral purposes and programmes; as they develop common moral purposes and programmes they are more likely to listen to each other.

What this means for modern societies and in particular 'the powers that be'

Alec Dickson once said that one of the profoundest questions before modern societies is 'How do we enable young people to feel needed?' There can be little quarrel with that general statement, but it could not be allowed to stand alone. 'Needed for what?' has to be added. There have been philosophers in previous ages who argued that slaves were needed by the economy. Nobody, of course, will admit to seeing the young to be needed as 'hewers of wood and drawers of water', but it may be found on investigation that those who speak of the young people as being needed are casting them for a role in which they are simply required to endorse the present system.

In modern societies strong support should be given to those educational agencies and processes which neither indoctrinate nor disinherit the young, which recognize the peril of the 'half-emancipated' who may be more frustrated and destructive than the enslaved, which realize that it is not simply an 'either-or' position where they require more freedom or more support but that in some respects they may need more support and in others more freedom, which are interested not merely in the fact, but also in the quality, of communication between the generations. In short, support should be given to the educational forces which speak for society to the young and challenge them to share a destiny with the rest of us which without them is not fully defined.

It is relatively easy to describe the objectives as we see them. 'Teach social responsibility without indoctrination and with no unnecessary social control.' In terms of our previous equation, can $S+$ be made to equal $R+$ and $I-$ through our better sociological knowledge, social engineering skill and human concern?

What this means for older people

The view we have expressed previously about the 'correct' attitude of adults to the young is based partly on many conversations in which young people have expressed their disappointment with adult attitudes to them. They frequently complain that they are patronized. 'Our parents never discuss anything serious with us,' said a group of teenage girls to an educational officer of the Marriage Guidance Council. 'They treat us like kids' is of course a common complaint. But through all these conversations when they are complaining it is not most frequently about the lack of freedom: what they want most – though they cannot always put it into words – is to be treated seriously as members of the community, junior partners of older people, with all that involves in terms of respect, expectation and affection.

When the issue is put to them, that is what most adults will say they want to be for the rising generation: what self-respecting parent or teacher, for example, would say other? But the danger is that lip-service only will be paid to the idea: as in much else, the peril is not in a denial but in a counterfeit, the false imitation that deceives by resemblance. Many adults in this matter resemble authoritarian discussion-group leaders who are trying self-consciously to work with non-directive methods. They allow the group to have a free discussion and at the end of session, say in so many words, 'Now the game is over. I will tell you the truth of this matter.' So, many of us subscribe to these notions: we may go through the motions of putting them into practice, but the inner intention is not there nor do we 'expect and respect'. That adults should always or even frequently govern their relationships with the young by any predetermined notion is a horrible idea, whose practical application would destroy the natural spontaneities which should characterize the relationship. But it is the almost complete absence of the 'expect and respect' approach which marks many relationships across the generational gap. Positively, it can be the 'water-mark' of many natural and spontaneous encounters.

What this means for the young people

Many young people do not show any strong feeling that they have a duty to the community, which is just another way of saying, that they do not appear to have any strong feelings of obligation to the people as a whole living in the same country as themselves. (This does not contradict our earlier view that the desire to serve may be just below the surface.) One reason for this may well be that they have passed through an educational system which, properly concerned to be child-centred, thereby failed to be 'community-related', that is, omitted to teach children that they owed something to the society which had nourished them. Many of them also have not been entirely unaffected by the persuasive voices in our day seeking to convince them that 'society' is to blame for all their ills. (Is ours the first generation that to a marked degree has found the scapegoat not in a social or ethnic group, but in society itself?) The extreme examples of these effects are found among those youngsters who have been oversold on the facts of a society's exploitation of individual members, who see only their rights and the rights of those like them and none of their duties associated with living in a human society. Perhaps the *reductio ad absurdum* example is the anarchists demonstrating for the overthrow or destruction of society, who, when one of their number is injuired in a brawl, grumbles because the ambulance is three minutes late in arriving. They conveniently forget that the ambulance is provided by the society, the association of human beings, which they affect to despise.

At less nonsensical levels one often finds youth confused and personally judges them to be wrong about their attitudes to the community. The writer once took part in a university teach-in on students' grants. Several speakers emphatically made the point that there was no cause for gratitude, either way, between country and student since it was a simple contract: the country required educated people and the students wanted an education. They did not take kindly to the comment that a contract – as in marriage – need not necessarily exclude gratitude both ways.

Where this attitude prevails, it is in fact possible to blame society in the single sense that there are not nearly enough voices stressing duties to the community as well as rights. Recent books on the social education of the young have concentrated almost entirely on individual development, and the duty of the society to the youngster, as though there can somehow be a society without people to compose it, as though there can be, for example, a compassionate society without people of compassion.

This is not intended as an argument for multiplying youthful conformists; they are to be welcomed as agents of change though not of destruction; they should learn what may be appreciated before they start to criticize and grasp an idea of the scope of community caring today about which they often know very little unless they are personally involved or until one part of the social services comes in for severe public criticism. A society like ours supports as well as restrains: it offers a measure of succour even to the most deprived. In the long run the maintenance and extension of its caring depends upon the extent to which its citizens are 'community-minded' and 'community-involved'.

Is voluntary community service by young people the answer?

The growth of voluntary service for the community by young people during the last ten years has gone largely unnoticed by the general public.[6] A multiplicity of organizations reflects the expansion. There are the older groups concerned with service overseas like International Volunteer Service and Voluntary Service Overseas; there are the newer national groups concerned with service in the country like Community Voluntary Service and the Young Volunteer Force (which received government backing and is at work in several local authority areas); and there are local varieties of the same movement like Young Volunteers of Merseyside,

Youth Action Sheffield, Bristol's Service G, Task Force in eight London boroughs, Manchester's Youth and Community Service, Birmingham's Young Volunteers' Trust and at least a dozen others.

The organizers can usually report an overwhelming response from the young people and it frequently appears that there are more volunteers than available jobs to go round. 'When International Voluntary Service mobilized its forces on both sides of the Channel to work on the beaches threatened by the *Torrey Canyon* no public authority could be found to accept their volunteers' (Alec Dickson). Task Force recruited 11,000 young people in the London area to visit the old and lonely.

There are appealing features of the developments of the movement apart from its expansion of numbers. One is that it has ceased to be only a leisure-time activity for those who have left school. More and more schools are including voluntary service on the curriculum for older pupils. It has also in many places become part of the training for police cadets. For community service to become an integral part of the educational system would accord well with the argument of this book, though—to anticipate a future argument – active involvement should represent as far as possible a genuinely free choice.

Nor can one fail to be stirred by the variety of jobs the young people undertake nor the amount of imagination and ingenuity they often display. 'Sixth forms have conducted debates in psychiatric wards to secure audience-participation and girls have ventured into Asian homes to teach conversational English to Pakistani women in Huddersfield,' says Alec Dickson. From the same source comes the story of a teacher and 14–15-year-old children from a Lancashire school. How could they help with the problem of old people living alone who might be taken ill and not be able to signal for help from outside? After weeks of fruitless experimentation, they bought a time-switch that could be set to give a signal after a predetermined passage of time. But how to prevent the signal being given unnecessarily? Finally they had the answer: every time the lavatory plug is pulled the arm of the time switch is returned to zero.

Moreover, when every allowance is made for the impressionistic nature of speeches made by enthusiasts, it is clear that voluntary service has provided for many young people taking part, a signi-

ficant experience and one that prepares them for general and specific roles as adults in society. 'What,' asks James Grigg, 'could be of
greater value to a budding policeman than to do a stint among
juvenile delinquents, or in some other milieu where he is brought
up against the problems of modern society?' Of the work of the
fifty girls from a Sheffield secondary school who fed handicapped
patients in a long-stay ward, the comment was made, 'What was
previously a shovelling operation became a labour of love – and
half a hundred girls now feel that their city has need of them.'

There is enough evidence to suggest that young people will
respond materially to a cry for help from their community. Confirmation comes from elsewhere.[7]

> Kennedy himself advanced the idea of a 'Youth Peace
> Corps' a little tentatively during the campaign – it was
> mid-October and two in the morning – to an audience of
> students at the University of Michigan. The result was
> unexpectedly warm. A few days later a Michigan delegation
> greeted Kennedy at Toledo with a petition signed by several
> hundred prospective volunteers.

But there is a debit side and the enthusiasts for voluntary work
by young people should listen carefully to their critics.[8] The enterprise comes under fire on the following grounds:

a That it is often a form of cheap labour, in many cases a sub-
stitute for professional social-personal services which the country
is not civilized enough to provide at public expense.
b That it is middle class in outlook since it encourages service by
the privileged for the unprivileged.
c That it is paternalistic, producing many situations in which
older people decide what it is appropriate for the young to do.
d That it fails to encourage young people to think critically of
their society and ask what needs to be changed in it: the assumption of their offer is to accept society as it is and give personal
service rather than be involved in necessary political action.

To be fair, the founding fathers of these movements are aware
of these criticisms. They themselves would see voluntary service
as the transition from the Welfare State to the Participant Society:
it is not unknown of course for organizations to reflect not too
accurately the stated goals of their leaders. But as voluntary service
by the young has worked out at the local level it has often earned

these criticisms: it has too often proved to be a case of older people choosing jobs for young people, and not always on any broader basis than 'the devil finds work for idle hands to do and isn't it lovely to see those young people doing something for somebody else for nothing and it doesn't matter particularly what they do'; it has sometimes been paternalistic and a contemporary example of middle-class 'do-goodery'; it has not always asked young people to have any hand in the definition of community goals and needs and to plan personal service or political action as they think is required. Where local efforts have been of this nature, they have certainly not fulfilled our earlier demand for a moral dialogue between older and young people and the discovery of mutually-acceptable moral tasks.

If local practice continues to move closer to the stated aims of these movements, then voluntary service contains a large promise that youngsters may come to accept more responsibility for others and hence for the community, and this improvement would seem to qualify the efforts for more support from public funds.

But will even an improved, expanded and better-supported scheme of voluntary service be enough of itself to teach community responsibility and involvement to a new generation? We think not. Impressive as the numbers are, they cater for no more than a minority of any age-group. In appealing to a wider constituency, they are likely to encounter one formidable difficulty, and that is the obstinate attitudes of 'those who care for none of these things' because in other parts of their education – at school and home, for example – a good case has not been made to them for community involvement. So we turn to a suggestion, popular in many quarters, which is believed to meet this objection.

Is compulsory national community service the answer?

A distinguished brigadier recently claimed[9] that a survey he conducted suggests that a large majority of the people in this country are in favour of the return of national service. His questions went to a 20,000 cross-section of the public from ages sixteen to seventy. The results showed that 84 per cent would welcome the introduction of conscription for military service or community work. The brigadier admitted that those who are more solidly in favour tend to be in the age-group thirty and upwards.

The advocates of this solution to the 'youth problem' are more commonly found to be arguing in favour of conscription for community service, not military service and this is partly because the military authorities, despite the present difficulties of recruitment to the forces, do not feel that under modern conditions, the best contribution is made to our defensive position by the return of national service.

The summary dismissal of these proposals is justified here on the grounds that they are not in any case politically feasible. No political party seeking power is likely to include them in their programme for some time at least. Linked with this is the fact that they probably underestimate the number of young people who would 'tear up their draft cards'. Nor do these advocates always seem aware of the costly and complex administrative machinery that such a scheme requires.

Apart from the political feasibility of national service for community work, there are other serious objections, the main one being the effects of compulsion. Most enthusiasts for this solution support their case by citing the success of schemes for voluntary service by young people in this country over the last decade. They do not always appreciate how decisive in their development has usually been the fact that it is what the young people, to some extent, have chosen themselves to do. The movement would lose a lot of power if this was replaced by compulsion. We should understand by reflecting upon our own experience: most of us have far more enthusiasm and energy for those tasks in which we have chosen to engage.

For these reasons it appears better to seek more support for voluntary schemes as well as to improve the quality of the service at local level in ways which have already been indicated. There is much evidence to support this view. Part of it is that it has usually been found that many more young people wish to take part in voluntary community service than can be catered for by the present administration and opportunities. A poll conducted by the *Daily Mail* a few years ago showed that 74 per cent of those between the ages of 16 and 20 felt that they were not doing enough for the community.

But to repeat a previous point, voluntary service movements are not enough of themselves to bring together Britain's need for the involvement with the community of the young and the felt need of many young people to be more involved with their community: the emphasis and opportunity should be present in other educational contacts. The Bill which the Bishop of Norwich presented to the House of Lords a few years ago sought to cover both these points: 'That this House calls upon Her Majesty's Government to put forward to all young people a programme of voluntary service to the community as an integral part of their education, taking into account their wishes as shown in a recent opinion poll.'

Can a pluralistic society have common goals?

Unless the phrase had become a shuttlecock in the political game, we should say that our plea is simply for a society which offers to its young at more and more places opportunities for 'responsibility and freedom'. The argument we repeat is that both realities are important for community and young alike. The community needs the involvement of young people and they need it too for significance and identity. Unless the young are given the possibilities of freedom they are degraded and humiliated. And a modern society, especially at a time of rapid social change, needs citizens who are 'free'. 'The greatest creative ages have tended to be those in which reasoned dissent was welcome.'[10]

But now before considering the practical application of these ideas to specific areas of educational effort, we face what may be for many a considerable objection to this total approach. In appealing for the discovery of common social goals and moral tasks for people of all ages in Britain, are we not in danger of overlooking a formidable reality to which previous reference has been made, that is that in our country today we are in a position of 'anomie' one aspect of which is that the old value-systems which 'united' the people are no longer so widely accepted? Many people would put the issue in simpler terms. 'Britain is no longer a Christian country. When it was there was a principle of unity and social control. And nothing so far has arisen to take its place.'

One symptom of this is the diminishing role of the churches. 'There is, however, a good deal of evidence other than the decline in church attendance to suggest that religious forces exercise less influence over people's lives than they did . . . Fewer people give less of their time and attention to religious thought and action. Today the voice of religion is small if not yet still.'[11] But more is involved. There is a suspicion, expressed articulately by certain writers but held vaguely in the minds of many more people, that 'every ideology is a conspiracy'. Widespread is the conviction that there is not one interpretation of any of the major questions which can be imposed on everybody, and that people who act as though there were, are, consciously or unconsciously, serving their own interests in one way or another.

Solidarity and co-operative efforts within large human groups like nations are most frequently associated with one or more of three realities.

a A common faith. There is a direct link between unity and the extent to which the individual members of the group have internalized a common set of values. The members of a monastery, of a small nation struggling for national freedom, of a group fighting for a political reform and of a church are obviously more likely to be seeking common ends than those not similarly associated.[12]

b A common threat. Human groups of all sizes develop strong feelings of common identity and pursuits when they are felt to be threatened by outside forces. Modern dictators have understood this well and have used their knowledge to foster a spirit of national unity. In a city under siege many private quarrels and party factions may be forgotten for the time being. 'The Dunkirk spirit' still lives in the British memory: it is said to have been a time when class barriers were removed.

c A charismatic leader. Large human groups may be unified in purpose and outlook by allegiance to a leader who is admired, loved, depended upon and obeyed by all. One man in himself may express the hopes and calm the fears of a whole nation. History contains many examples.

None of these requirements is markedly fulfilled in contemporary British society. As to the first we are not aware of a British way of life, distinctive from the rest and supported by a set of beliefs: we may in fact have to travel abroad before we find ourselves admired for virtues like moderation and tolerance. As to the second, we may be threatened by all sorts of outside dangers but it certainly does not form part of our daily consciousness. As regards the third, there has been no such leader in Britain since Winston Churchill, more than a quarter of a century ago.

In fact, the challenge which faces a sophisticated democracy is to discover community goals and moral tasks unsupported by the 'myths' of religion or national uniqueness which always seem to have been necessary in the past. A democracy should work at the task, difficult though not impossible, of defining humane aims without an 'ideology'. Indeed it could be argued that many conversations about right and wrong become confused when they are associated with ideologies: the real issue becomes obscured and the struggle becomes symbolic. One still meets Russians and Americans who cannot see any good in anything that the other does.

But let us take the most recurring example in British life today. It is, I think, a pity that almost all the moral education which is carried on in this country is associated with religious beliefs and assumptions.[13] Whatever the merits in the argument about the inevitable link between religion and morality, we cannot in practice continue this association always and everywhere. In the present climate of opinion, we are compelled to offer moral teaching that does not always come in a religious wrapping, since the wrapping is now unacceptable to many. But the 'religious lobby' in this country is still powerful. They are usually found to be arguing that the two must go together and not invariably are they prepared to work with people who seek similar humane ends but with different sanctions and assumptions. 'Anomie' need not lead to moral relativism and confusion, though it offers a severe test of our maturity.

It is time that we gave a few examples of what is meant by our society discovering a degree of unity and purpose by the sharing of community goals and moral tasks, with no necessary doctrinal underpinning, and how in particular this can contribute to young people experiencing at the same time more freedom and responsibility. These could be supplied in general terms like the statements, 'Tolerance is always better than bigotry'; 'Modern societies grow more civilized as they care for the weak and unprotected and power is shared by more people.' But this does not appeal as being so useful an exercise as the examination of one or two specific contemporary questions which can be material for moral conversation between the generations.

One is the challenge to build in Britain a genuinely multi-racial society, where for people of whatever coloured skin or racial origin there is equal opportunity, mutual tolerance and cultural diversity. The main motivations for this optimistic enterprise for many people still are religious, an extension into the modern industrialized country of the long-standing missionary motive, 'Christ died for every man' (of whatever colour implied). Now it happens that my private judgment agrees with this. But we cannot – and in my view we have no right to – make this assumption with those, including the young, who do not share this point of view. What then? We should discover other grounds for a case for civilized behaviour, and these are not far to find as a basis for discussion. For example, we can discuss the proposition in terms of human rights: that everybody has a right to his life. Or going further we may say that we should consider the proposition that if we devalue any other human being we ultimately devalue ourselves. Most young people are in fact interested in these kinds of conversations and often feel when the dialogue is initiated by adults who do not want to patronize them, that they are being taken seriously at last. But 'moral conversations' are not exhausted by a disclosure of ideal intentions: they go on to explore the difficulties of and objections to the ideas. (Perhaps the worst effects of speeches by 'racialists' in Britain is that they pre-empt discussions about the real problems of having an 'immigrant population'.) But there is more to do than talk or listen – it is not enough to be right, we have to ask how we might win : there can be shared tasks as well as shared ideas.

Too often when adults begin to initiate conversations of this kind, they are expected to come with a set of conventional ideas about right and wrong which must be received as the legacy of a vanished world. But the fact is that all of us living in our world are faced by dilemmas which turn out to be moral in character, some of them new in form but nearly all of them new in their intensity and dimension. The survival of the human race is threatened from three directions: man's destruction of his own physical environment; overpopulation; hydrogen bomb warfare. How far should technology be allowed to go? When do human values call a halt? The truth is we are all, young and old alike, 'in the same boat'. And though it may currently be said that about some of these vast problems there is precisely nothing that any one individual can do, that is not true of all of them; and if we cannot affect events, there is something essentially human in helping one another to understand our predicament.

A slightly different kind of 'moral conversation' that can arise

9

across the generations and that has been proved in the writer's experience to have value on occasions is where we are trying to understand together what purpose was served by *mores* which we have inherited from the past, even when it is open to question whether those *mores* have present relevance, at least in the form in which they come to us. It is unlikely that any long-standing norm served no useful purpose for societies and individuals, nor will it do simply to say that they served the vested interests of one section since this appears not to explain why they were accepted by the majority. One example is the norm of sexual behaviour which still expects people to be loyal to their marriage vows and sets its face against extra-marital sexual activity. Now it may be true that there are in our society more and more people who in their private lives are disregarding this norm. It is also debatable whether this norm can be expected to survive unchanged into the future. But what is not in dispute is that it did not grow up fortuitously in many human societies, say because a committee of curates passed a law on a quiet Sunday afternoon. Presumably men and women found that the game was less dangerous and more hopeful of happiness if there were rules; in this case perhaps that children should be nourished and nurtured, women not abandoned and both men and women find emotional support – all of which is important for societies as it is for individuals. Before we dismiss any traditional standard of behaviour, we ought to ask what purpose it served, what was its intention, and then go on to ask whether the same need exists today and if so, how is it to be served.[14] What is depressingly absent from the conversation of some young people is any appreciation of the intention of those very standards from the past which they propose to throw overboard as old-fashioned.[15]

The last section was concerned to argue, that even without a 'myth' and in a situation of 'anomie', it is worth trying to use conversations about contemporary moral problems as part of the support for 'better' relationships between older and younger people, and, generally between young people and the rest of organized society. It is hoped that none of this argument has given an impression of glibness. Admittedly many of the problems we have indicated prove to be complex and not completely soluble.

There is no suggestion here of a panacea: nothing, we repeat, will produce the instant 'mature society'. Sometimes there is integrated action which can follow our conversations, but even where this is not a possibility our argument is that much has been gained, not least in the realm of inter-generational relationships.

When we come to examine specific areas where our central notion could be given practical application, we need to remind ourselves once more that what is being offered is not a blue-print appropriate to every situation where the young and old meet. We need to test out the possibilities in different situations. How feasible is it for older people on behalf of their society to be offering young people 'permission and support and a cry for help'? And how far the notion can be carried will depend upon many factors, not the least being the experiences of the young people with older people in other settings. This can prove a formidable restriction affecting seriously the expectations which the young bring and the identity which they give to older people.

It is possible however to provide at this point four documentary illustrations – two negative on 'how not to do it' – and two positive on 'how to do it'.

In 1968 the rebel students at Hornsey College of Art in North London occupied the college, began a radical reconstruction of art education and set up what they called the Crouch End Commune. One is not necessarily defending their actions: it is the outcome which is most interesting. In fact they found that the experience had larger implications for art education than it had for politics. Thus their report includes the following. 'It was in the small seminars of not more than twenty people that ideas could be thrashed out. Each person felt personally involved in the dialogue and felt the responsibility to respond vociferously to anything that was said. These discussions often went on to the small hours of the morning. If only such a situation were possible under "normal" conditions.'[16] In our terms, the educational experience could have been the basis of discussion between the young and their elders, but it tended to be lost in the bitterness of the confrontation. A local newspaper commented:[17]

a bunch of crackpots, here in Haringey, or in Grosvenor
Square, or Paris, or Berlin, or Mexico, can never overthrow
an established system. The lesson is there, staring the students

in the face, although it may well take some time to penetrate through to their minds. They may dislike having to conform to a system in which they are required to study, and follow set programmes, and take examinations or their equivalents: and acknowledging that in doing so they are through the indulgence of others preparing themselves for a lifetime of earning, but the mere fact that they do so is not enough to alter the system. The system is ours. We the ordinary people, the nine-to-five, Monday-to-Friday, semi-detached, suburban wage-earners, we are the system. We are not the victims of it. We are not the slaves of it. We are it, and we like it. Does any bunch of twopenny-halfpenny kids think they can turn us upside down? They'll learn.

The second negative documentary example takes us back a decade to the Cuban crisis. At this time an organizer visited a youth club in the Midlands. As she entered the door she heard youngsters discussing the situation in a slightly frightened and rather confused way. 'It could mean annihilation,' said one. Arrived at the leader's office the organizer commented on what she had heard and wondered whether the members could have a discussion on the subject that night as it seemed so important to them. The leader's reply was curious – and startling. 'It's impossible I'm afraid. We have our discussion group on Friday nights.' (It was Wednesday.)

By hopeful contrast there is in the Midlands, in a working-class area, a well attended youth centre which organizes regular Sunday seminars on public issues for its members. On a recent Sunday there was an attendance of eighty. A speaker who is an expert on the chosen subject is invited but most of the time is spent in discussion groups.

The second positive example is of a more generalized nature. It comes from some examples of 'detached youth work', that is where the professional youth worker is in the street not in a building, seeking to make contact with socially needy young people who would not of their own initiative join a youth organization. There are two written accounts[18] which demonstrate the opportunities in this kind of work for meeting youngsters on their own ground whilst going on to help them to discover other sets of values which are worth their consideration.

Schools

What part could schools play in the type of social education which is our plea? Is it any different from the part they are playing now? We touch here on a subject about which there are many different and deeply-held views but the following are, it seems, features of a pertinent discussion.

Has our educational philosophy become too child-centred? (Many theorists would deny that it has become so significantly in practice and still see it as 'subject orientated', authoritarian and dedicated to social control.) Are we in danger of producing a nation of individualists? Should not the balance be redressed by an emphasis on community responsibility? Despite the lowering of the voting age to eighteen, the movement to have some form of political education in schools is the enthusiasm of a few like Professor Bernard Crick, formerly of Sheffield University, now of Birkbeck College, London.

Is there not a tendency to restrict the socialization process in the schools to socialization to accept things as they are, to produce in other words conformists rather than constructive revolutionaries, people well adapted to live in stable times but not in an era of rapid social change? Many books on the subject of education see the end product of the school process as passive partners in a traditional society, rather than active partners in necessary change.[19]

Many teachers, particularly in 'rough' areas would consider our hope naïve and unrealistic: the struggle to retain social control with large classes and inadequate equipment, and perhaps in a nineteenth-century building, leaves little room for the fulfilment of these dreams. Those of us who are not subject to these daily pressures would be wise not to speak too emphatically here. Yet one has seen schools in these circumstances, subject to neighbourhood pressures that are not invariably helpful, and whilst retaining the structure of adult power necessary for control, where there seems to be an understanding that education includes an invitation to active partnership in the community.

Churches

We entertain high hopes of moral fellowships. It is true that the churches together undertake a volume of the social education of the young which is not always widely appreciated. Moreover they have several common advantages in the educational process: one in that they have local branches and international connections; another is that they are associations of all age-groups and do not necessarily segregate the adolescents from others.

But from our point of view they may display several vulnerabilities. In the light of a previous discussion, they are sometimes tempted to be 'indoctrinators' so concerned to push the 'Truth' down the youngster's throat that they do not give him time to digest it; sometimes they are 'recruiters' primarily seeking supporters for their institutions. Their proper pastoral concern may blind them to the influence of social and political pressures on the individual. The same pastoral concern often makes them over-protective of the young.

However, in language that they would understand, the sins of omission are more serious than the sins of commission. Local congregations do not frequently provide opportunities for the kind of confrontation between young and old which we have approved: in fact, work among children and young people tends to be the concern of a few rather than the whole organized local church. Similarly, it is rare to find them interpreting community involvement as a dimension of Christian obedience.[20] To put one illustration briefly, they are likely to produce more church wardens than county councillors – and to talk about having done so.

Political institutions

Here the moral content of the discussion appears to be at a low level though all factions will maintain that there are moral reasons for their arguments. On investigation however it is usually found that these are being used to support a case, and are not decisive. Politics is a serious matter about moral questions but too often it is corrupted by politicians until it is primarily about power, prestige and personalities. This is precisely one reason why some young people have lost faith in our present political structures. A few politicians genuinely respect the opinions of the young, but they are not usually found holding high office. Fresh ideas from the youth sections of political parties are often treated with suspicion. They are too often seen as there to receive a truth, to give support and to swell the ranks.

It may be thought that in asking for the application of our principle to political organizations we are asking the impossible, but the campaigning tactics of Eugene McCarthy in the USA a few years ago, showed that this approach will gain a response, and a long delay in this experiment is likely to drive more and more young people either into extreme revolutionary affiliations or deeper political apathy.

The mass-media of communication

There are many popular illusions here. A completely 'free Press' for example is a myth. What a paper says is partly decided by thoughts of circulation, just as popularity ratings have a decisive hand in what appears on the television screen. The law provides further restrictions, as does also what is likely to be repugnant to the accepted norms of the society, like democratic sentiments. For example, even before recent legislation, it was unlikely that any sound or television programme would pronounce in favour, even mildly, of racial discrimination.

If the mass-media cannot be neutral on major issues, perhaps we may hope that one day positive and creative relationships between the generations may receive more emphatic support. There have certainly been some programmes which – out of deference to the demands of show-business – have exacerbated conflict between the young and their society rather than helped us to work it out in creative ways.

To labour the obvious, young people are educated to be mature, responsible, discriminating members of their community not only through contact with official, organized forms of education, but by every contact that they have with older people. Most adults are constantly brought into contact with young people in several places, including home and work. And as we are basically concerned here with a change in adult attitudes, we may not confine our attention to professional educationalists and sociologists. Democratic machinery does not, we repeat, guarantee the democratic process; we need more adults who will see the young as active partners in an enterprise not yet fully defined.

So the reader is invited to pass in review the young people

between fifteen and twenty-five personally known to him or her. They may be our own children, or apprentices, office-boys, trainees or juvenile workers at our place of employment; they may be young people we teach; or we may think of the youth who delivers our newspaper every morning and with whom we often just have the fleeting opportunity to pass the time of day.

How do we think of them? Are they primarily enemies, puzzles, children or strangers? How do we behave towards them? Happily we may say there are many aspects of our relationship – teasing, guiding, quarrelling and reprimanding. But on our side are the following four elements included?

1 Permission. Do we want to control them too much? Do we appreciate their need to work things out for themselves? Do we feel even about our own children that they are their own people and we would like to get to know them?

2 Support. Their inexperience makes them vulnerable in certain areas and they may need help from us and not always be able to put the request into words.

3 Partners with us in common enterprises. We have things to do together though they will be many things we shall do separately.

4 Partners who will have their own ideas of what is to be done and how it is to be done.

Notes

1 A. Etzioni, *The Active Society*, The Free Press, New York, 1968.
2 Cf. bibliography at the end of this chapter for books on the subject of community development.
3 Kingsley Davis, *Human Society*, MacMillan, 1948, p. 230.
4 *Fifteen to Eighteen* (The Crowther Report), Central Advisory Council for Education (England), HMSO, 1959.
5 Kenneth Keniston, 'Social Change and Youth in America' in *Youth: Change and Challenge*, Basic Books, 1963.
6 Among the relatively few press notices are the following: *Observer* colour supplement, 6 November 1966, 'The Young Volunteers'.
   Guardian 2 May 1967, 'Crusaders without a cause', Alec Dickson. Cf. *New Society* 8 May 1969, p. 716 for a discussion about the functions of the Young Volunteers Force Foundation.
7 Arthur M. Schlesinger, Jr., *A Thousand Days. John F. Kennedy in the White House*, André Deutsch, 1965, p. 527.
8 Bernard D. Davies is one of the most articulate critics, cf. *New*

Society 24 August 1967, pp. 258–9. 'An attempt to tame the young.' For another, unsigned criticism of the Young Volunteers Force Foundation cf. *New Society* 23 November 1968: 'the new scheme may indeed recruit a few thousand middle-class youngsters to a middle-class cause, but it will do nothing to help youth work change its image as a juvenile service for a committed minority and may even reinforce this.'

9 Reported in *Mobilization of Youth: Voluntary Service or Conscription?*, report of a seminar held at the Royal United Service Institution 28 January 1970, published by the Royal United Service Institution, Whitehall.

10 J. Bronowski and Bruce Mazlish, *The Western Intellectual Tradition*, Penguin Books.

11 Bryan Wilson, *Religion in Secular Society*, Penguin Books, pp. 24–5.

12 Cf. Margaret Phillips, *Small Social Groups in England*, Methuen, 1965, chapter 11.

13 Perhaps it is not inappropriate to give my own position here. I am a member of a church and cherish the Christian hope. But this is a matter of private judgment. And I think we have passed the point when we can through statutory agencies impose the Christian interpretation – an approach which is particularly unhelpful when we seem to be saying, 'moral education within a religious framework or no moral education'. I do not find this creates any further intellectual difficulties for me in the acceptance of Christianity. We have to learn to distinguish between secularization – which can mean that it is foolish to rely upon God to do for us what we have to do for ourselves – and secularism – which dismisses the whole idea of God as an irrelevance, and possibly a dangerous one at that. (Cf. Harvey Cox, *The Secular City*, Penguin Books). But this is a large subject and further discussion here is not fitting.

14 For a discussion of this point in relation to Christian ethics, cf. John A. T. Robinson, *Christian Freedom in a Permissive Society*, S.C.M. Press, 1970, 32, e.g. 'only the man who knows he cannot lose what the Sabbath stands for can afford to criticize it radically.'

15 For further reflection upon the main point of this section, the following are two useful sources –
Community Work and Social Change, Gulbenkian Foundation Report, Longmans, 1968, pp. 4–5, 'The purpose of community work in its wider context'.
C. Wright Mills, *The Sociological Imagination*, Penguin Books, chapter 1.

16 Students and Staff of Hornsey College of Art, 'The Hornsey Affair', p. 38.
17 Ibid., p. 207.
18 Mary Morse, *The Unattached*, Penguin Books.
    G. Goetschius and J. Tash, *Working with Unattached Youth*, Routledge & Kegan Paul, 1967.
19 This is, in general, a defect in an otherwise excellent book on the subject by M. D. Shipman, *Sociology of the School*, Longmans, 1968.
20 I have dealt with this issue at greater length in a booklet, *Church, Youth and Community Development*, Chester House Publications, 1970.

Suggestions for further reading

Democracy and Community Development

Batten, T. R., *Non-directive Approaches in Group and Community Work*, Oxford University Press, 1967.
Butler, D. E., *The Study of Political Behaviour*, Hutchinson, 1966.
Collier, K. G., *The Social Purpose of Education : Personal and Social Values in Education*, Routledge & Kegan Paul, 1959.
Fromm, Erich, *The Fear of Freedom*, Routledge & Kegan Paul, 1942.
Gulbenkian Foundation, *Community Work and Social Change*, Longmans, 1968.
Murray, Ross and Lappin, B. W., *Community Organization : Theory, Principles and Practice*, Harper & Row, 1967.
Leaper, R. A. B., *Community Work*, N.C.S.S.
Musgrave, P. W., *Society and Education in England since 1800*, Methuen, 1968.
Ottaway, A. K. C., *Education and Society : An Introduction to the Sociology of Education*, Routledge & Kegan Paul, 1953.

Education for Democracy

Batten, T. R., *The Human Factor in Community Work*, Oxford University Press, 1965.
Borer, M. C., *Citizenship*, Museum Press, 1962.
Central Advisory Council for Education (England), (Newsom Report) *Half our Future* (Newsom Report), HMSO, 1963.
Gillette, Arthur, *One Million Volunteers*, Penguin Books.
Judd, Frank, 'Community service: no deadening hand', *Guardian*, 4 October 1966.

Schools Council, *Society and the Young School Leaver,* Working
    Paper No. 11, 1969.
Vaizey, John, *Education for Tomorrow,* Penguin Books.
Youth Service Development Council, *Youth and Community Work in
    the 70s* (Fairbairn-Milson Report), HMSO 1970.

Programme suggestions for 'education for democracy'

Unfortunately there is a dearth of material under this heading and
what there is is set almost exclusively in the content of religious
assumptions. But the N.A.Y.C. pamphlets on political education are
useful, as are also the booklets published by the S.C.M. Press under
the general title of 'Thinking Things Through', particularly the
contributions by Eric Lord, No. 1, 'Getting on with people', and
No. 7, 'Take your choice'.

Index